THE FOOD MIX

C000052058

Also available

The Halogen Oven Cookbook
Slow Cooking Properly Explained
Slow Cooking: Best New Recipes
Pressure Cooking Properly Explained
Steaming
Fresh Bread in the Morning From Your Bread Machine
Ice Cream Made Easy

THE
FOOD MIXER
COOKBOOK

Norma Miller

A HOW TO BOOK

ROBINSON

First published in Great Britain in 2010 by Robinson

5 7 9 10 8 6

A CIP catalogue record for this book
is available from the British Library.

ISBN 978-0-7160-2264-0 (paperback)

Printed and bound by CPI Group (UK) Ltd, Croydon, CR0 4YY

Papers used by Robinson are from well-managed forests
and other responsible sources

Robinson
An imprint of
Little, Brown Book Group
Carmelite House
50 Victoria Embankment
London EC4Y 0DZ

An Hachette UK Company
www.hachette.co.uk

www.littlebrown.co.uk

How To Books are published by Robinson, an imprint of Little, Brown Book Group.
We welcome proposals from authors who have first-hand experience of their subjects.
Please set out the aims of your book, its target market and its suggested
contents in an email to Nikki.Read@howtobooks.co.uk

CONTENTS

ACKNOWLEDGEMENTS

Thanks to:
Photography by Lisa Simmons:
www.lisasimmonsphotography.com

The recipes in this book were developed using
an Andrew James food mixer:
Andrew James UK Ltd
www.andrewjamesworldwide.com

INTRODUCTION

No kitchen should be without a food mixer. There are so many good and useful things to be achieved with this indispensable kitchen accessory. With home cooking back in fashion, a food mixer is just what you need to reduce the initial effort required by many recipes. And your food mixer can also inspire and encourage you to try your hand at all sorts of dishes.

With a large food mixer, home-made cakes and pastries are easy and quick to make, and you can include children in the weighing and decorating. A food mixer means much more control over what you cook, and more control too over the choice and quality of ingredients. So you can, for example, take full advantage of the wide range of flours and sugars now available, and possibly have some extra to freeze.

The recipes in this book use the food mixer's blades/beaters to best effect, demonstrating their versatility, including their functions to whisk, whip, knead and mix. The recipes also reflect the wide range of basic ingredients available to the home cook.

With more than one hundred recipes to inspire you the coverage is enormous: fluffy mousses, sponge cakes, dough for bread making and home-made pasta, drinks, cake and biscuit mixes, crumb and pastry mixes, a variety of fillings, icings and frostings to finish off cakes and biscuits, a cheese tart, a courgette loaf, and much much more. There are traditional recipes with a new twist, there is sometimes a seasonal element and there are recipes to be used as the basis of novelty cakes and birthday cakes.

About the food mixer

The food mixer is supplied with a large bowl, three blades/beaters and detachable protective dust covers which fit on top of each beater. In the recipes I will refer to the blades/beaters as the dough blade, the whisk and the mixer blade. Collectively I call them the beaters.

The food mixer is easy to assemble for use. Move the lifting lever clockwise and lift up the upper housing cover. Put the prepared ingredients into the mixer bowl and turn into place. Attach a blade and dust cover to the blade connector by turning it in a clockwise direction until attached. Close the housing cover by turning the lifting lever clockwise and press down the upper housing cover.

The switch knob is labelled from left to right: 'P' – '0' – '1' – '2' – '3' – '4' –'5' and '6'.

'P' is the pulse setting. It can quickly be turned on and off to give a short burst of speed which is very useful to combine ingredients together quickly, but without prolonged mixing. Use for gathering pastry crumbs together, savoury mixes for burgers and stuffing mixtures.

'0' is the OFF setting. Always turn the switch knob to the '0' position before unplugging the mixer.

'1' – '6' is a range of speed settings from very low through to very high. See the suggested speed settings for each blade/beater below.

Important

- The maximum continuous operating/mixing time is about 4 minutes for each use. The food mixer then needs 5–10 minutes' cooling time before the next use.
- Don't overfill the mixer bowl otherwise it will overflow during mixing.
- As the ingredients are mixed they move to the sides of the bowl – if necessary scrape back down with a flexible spatula.
- Use eggs and fats at room temperature.

The mixer blade

- The maximum quantity of ingredients to be used is 1500 g/3 lb 6 oz.
- Use for mixing sponge cakes, rich fruit cakes, scones, pastries, sweet and savoury fillings, batters, shakes and cocktails.
- Start with speed 1 for 10–15 seconds, increase to speed 2 for another 10–15 seconds (the ingredients will have combined together) and increase to speed 3–4 for 1–3 minutes until the ingredients are mixed together.

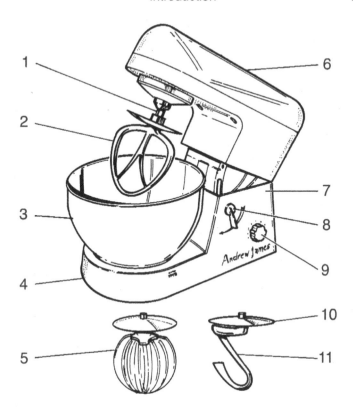

1. Blade connector
2. Mixer blade
3. Mixing bowl
4. Base of mixer
5. Whisk
6. Upper housing cover
7. Motor block
8. Lifting lever
9. Switch knob
10. Protective dust cover
11. Dough blade

The dough blade

- The maximum quantity of ingredients to be used is 1500 g/3 lb 6 oz.
- Use for mixing and kneading heavy mixes such as savoury and sweet bread doughs.
- Low speeds must be used with bread doughs as using a high speed would damage the machine. Start with speed 1 for 10–15 seconds, increase to speed 2 for another 10–15 seconds (the ingredients will have combined together) and increase to speed 3 for 1–3 minutes until the dough is kneaded and smooth.

The whisk

- To whisk egg whites for meringues the minimum number required is 4 large egg whites or 5 medium egg whites. There must be sufficient egg to reach the bottom of the whisk.
- Use for whipping eggs, egg whites and cream.
- Whisk egg whites on speed 4, 5 or 6 for up to 4 minutes until they are stiff.
- Whip 250 ml/9 fl oz cream on speed 4, 5 or 6 for up to 2–3 minutes or until the desired thickness is reached.

About the recipes

- All the recipes have been designed for using in a large food mixer. The preparation and cooking processes for each recipe are straightforward and easy to follow. To make things even easier, there are plenty of serving suggestions and hints and tips to go with the recipes.
- Many of the recipes can be doubled, but not halved as there needs to be enough mixture in the bowl to reach the blades.
- Save time by batch baking and freezing the excess.
- The recipes are often adaptable, and you can easily substitute interchangeable ingredients as you wish.
- For convenience, the recipe ingredients are listed in the order in which they are used. Though they are given in imperial as well as metric, you will find the metric measurements easier.
- All spoon measures are level unless otherwise stated.
- Some of the recipes can produce extra servings by doubling the quantities of ingredients – but make sure this increased volume still goes into your mixer bowl.
- Soft butter is used in some of the recipes; this is from the fridge.

- Where a recipe calls for boiling water, I have used a kettle and then added the boiling water to the recipe. This not only saves time but can save energy too.
- If you are preparing food for someone who has a food allergy be sure to study the list of ingredients carefully.
- A few recipes contain fresh chillies. Do take care when preparing them and remember to wash your hands thoroughly afterwards. Better still, wear rubber gloves while handling them.
- One or two recipes may contain raw or partly cooked eggs – please remember that it may be advisable to avoid eating these if you are pregnant, elderly, very young or sick.

About the ingredients
- I use a mixture of fresh seasonal produce, store-cupboard ingredients and canned or bottled foods, as well as some frozen items.
- My store cupboard always contains canned or bottled tomatoes, passata and a selection of canned beans, and small jars of pastes that are so quick and convenient – garlic, ginger, curry and chilli. Also a wide selection of spices and spice mixes. I prefer to use fresh herbs if possible. I also find it is useful to keep frozen peas and bags of mixed seafood in the freezer.
- Another favourite store-cupboard ingredient is liquid concentrated stock or vegetable bouillon powder. I particularly like using this because it is granular, and you can spoon out as much or as little as you want.
- Salt is kept to a minimum. Instead I prefer to source good quality ingredients that have bags of flavour. Often just a handful of freshly chopped herbs is all you need to boost flavour. Salt is included in some of the recipes, but use with discretion.
- If you are cooking for someone who has a food allergy be sure to study the list of ingredients carefully.

Equipment
- Large flexible spatulas are useful for scooping mixtures out of the bowl.
- I use a wide variety of pots and pans to cook my recipes in. In some of the baking recipes I give cake tin (metal) sizes and mention greasing and lining the tin. But if you are using flexible silicone bakeware you may not have to grease it. Look at the instruction leaflet. Remember to stand any flexible bakeware on a solid baking sheet.

Care and cleaning
- Read the 'important safety advice section' (see below).
- Always unplug the food mixer before cleaning.
- Turn the switch knob to the '0' position.
- Allow the mixer to cool down.
- Clean the exterior of the mixer with a damp cloth and a mild detergent.
- Do not get any water inside the machine. Never submerge the mixer in water.
- Wash the three blades and their protective dust covers by hand in hot water and a mild detergent. Do not put the beaters and dust covers in the dishwasher.
- The mixer bowl is dishwasher safe.
- Do not use any abrasive cleaners or scouring pads.

Important safety advice
Much of this advice should be common sense when using any kitchen appliance:

- When using a food mixer for the first time read the manufacturer's instruction manual.
- Important – The maximum continuous operating/mixing time is 4 minutes for each use. The food mixer then needs 5–10 minutes' cooling time before the next use.
- The maximum quantity of ingredients to be used is 1500 g/3 lb 6 oz.
- Don't overfill the mixer bowl otherwise it will overflow during mixing.
- The food mixer is very heavy and must be on a flat, stable heat-proof surface and not near the edge of work surfaces or near a heat source.
- Keep the surrounding areas clear and free from clutter.
- Never kink or clamp the mains lead.
- Make sure the power cord is not touching anything hot or hanging over the edge of a surface.
- Never leave the food mixer unattended whilst in use.
- Don't operate the mixer without ingredients in the mixer bowl.
- Use an appropriate speed setting for the lightness or density of the mixture.
- Keep hands away from the moving beaters.
- Switch the machine off when changing the beaters.

- Always unplug the food mixer before cleaning.
- Don't immerse the food mixer, power cord or electric plug in hot water or place in a dishwasher.
- Do not use out of doors.
- If any faults occur with your food mixer always contact the manufacturer.

1

BISCUITS AND COOKIES

With biscuits and cookies there is nothing like the real thing. And the real thing is to see your creations set out on baking trays, appetising and still warm, in a variety of shapes and sizes, and then to taste them, with all that anticipation built up since the ingredients first went into your trusty food mixer. The textures, soft or crisp, crunchy or chewy, and the flavours, cheesy, nutty or fruity, will be better than any other cookie or biscuit you can imagine.

Try as many as you fancy from this range of sweet and savoury recipes, including White Chocolate and Sour Cherry Cookies (see page 24), Lavender Shortbread (see page 22) and Sesame and Parmesan Wholemeal Nibbles (see page 27).

Apricot and Hazelnut Cookies

Use any of your favourite dried fruits and nuts in these mouthwatering cookies.

Makes about 20

140 g/5 oz dried ready-to-eat apricots
70 g/2½ oz hazelnut pieces
150 g/5½ oz self-raising flour
1 medium egg
½ tsp vanilla extract
115 g/4 oz soft butter
150 g/5½ oz soft light brown sugar

1. Attach the mixer blade to the mixer. Line 2–3 baking sheets with baking parchment (the cookies will spread). Preheat the oven to 180°C, Fan 165°C, Gas 4.
2. Roughly chop the apricots and hazelnuts. Sift the flour into a bowl and lightly mix the egg in a cup with the vanilla extract.
3. Put the butter and sugar into the mixer bowl. Mix on speed 1 or 2 for 10–20 seconds then increase the speed to 3–5 and mix until light and fluffy.
4. On a low speed, gradually add the egg to the butter mixture. Add the flour, half at a time, and then mix in the apricots and hazelnuts.
5. Put spoonfuls of the mixture onto the baking sheets leaving plenty of room for them to spread.
6. Put into the hot oven and bake for about 12–15 minutes until light golden brown.
7. Leave to cool on the tray for a minute or two, and then transfer to a wire rack to cool completely.

Spiced Lime Biscuits

A simple biscuit which is great for children to decorate, especially on festive occasions – cut into novelty shapes and decorate with icing, sweets, dried fruits and nuts.

Makes about 20

Oil for greasing
1 lime
350 g/12 oz plain flour
2 tsp ground mixed spice
1 medium egg
125 g/4½ oz soft butter
150 g/5½ oz caster sugar
70 g/2½ oz golden icing sugar

1. Attach the mixer blade to the mixer. Lightly grease a baking sheet. Preheat the oven to 180°C, Fan 165°C, Gas 4.
2. Finely grate the rind from the lime, cut in half and squeeze the juice from one half. Sift the flour and mixed spice into a bowl and break the egg into a cup.
3. Put the butter and caster sugar into the mixer bowl. Mix on speed 1 or 2 for 10–20 seconds then increase the speed to 3–5 and mix until light and fluffy.
4. On a low speed, gradually add the egg and grated lime to the butter mixture. Still on a low speed add the flour, half at a time, and use the pulse setting to gather the mixture together.
5. Turn the dough onto a lightly floured surface and gently knead until smooth. Roll out to a thickness of about 5 mm/¼ inch. Cut into rounds or shapes with biscuit cutters and lift onto the baking sheet spaced apart (cook them in batches). Re-roll the trimmings.
6. Put into the hot oven and bake for about 12–15 minutes until pale golden brown.
7. Leave to cool on the tray for a minute or two, and then transfer to a wire rack to cool completely.
8. Sift the icing sugar into a small bowl and stir in the lime juice a little at a time to give a thin flowing icing. With a small teaspoon drizzle a little icing over each biscuit and leave to set.

Coconut and Pineapple Discs

'Slice-and-bake dough'. Wrapped in foil, the dough will keep in the fridge for a few days. Just slice and bake when you feel the need for a biscuit.

Makes 30–40

Oil for greasing
250 g/9 oz plain flour
1 tsp baking powder
½ tsp ground cinnamon
1 large egg
60 g/2¼ oz dried ready-to-eat pineapple
150 g/5½ oz soft butter
175 g/6 oz caster sugar
60 g/2¼ oz desiccated coconut
Milk if necessary

1. Attach the mixer blade to the mixer. Lightly grease a baking sheet. Preheat the oven to 180°C, Fan 165°C, Gas 4.
2. Sift the flour, baking powder and cinnamon into a bowl. Break the egg into a cup and finely chop the pineapple.
3. Put the butter and sugar into the mixer bowl. Mix on speed 1 or 2 for 10–20 seconds, then increase the speed to 3–5 and mix until light and fluffy.
4. On a low speed, gradually add the egg to the butter mixture. Still on a low speed add the flour mixture and coconut, half at a time. When thoroughly mixed in, add the chopped pineapple and use the pulse setting to gather the mixture together. The mixture should be stiff, but if too dry mix in a little milk.
5. Turn the biscuit dough onto a sheet of foil and roll into a sausage shape about 5 cm/2 inches in diameter. Wrap in foil and chill for 1 hour until firm.
6. Open the foil and with a sharp knife cut 5 mm/¼ inch thick slices, as many as you want, and lift onto the baking sheet spaced apart. Keep the remaining dough wrapped in foil and chilled for up to a week, slice and bake as needed.
7. Put into the hot oven and bake for about 12–15 minutes until pale golden brown.
8. Leave to cool on the baking sheet for a minute or two, and then transfer to a wire rack to cool completely.

Almond Macaroons

Traditionally macaroons are baked on sheets of edible rice paper which is available in many food stores. When whisking egg whites, the mixer bowl and the whisk must be absolutely grease-free. Make small macaroons and dip in or sandwich together with melted chocolate. A tin of them would make a lovely gift.

Makes about 25–35

Rice paper
100 g/3½ oz glacé cherries
5 tsp ground rice
225 g/8 oz ground almonds
280 g/10 oz caster sugar
4 large or 5 medium egg whites
40 g/1½ oz flaked almonds

1. Attach the whisk to the mixer. Line 2–3 baking sheets with rice paper or baking parchment. Preheat the oven to 160°C, Fan 145°C, Gas 3.
2. Quarter each glacé cherry. Put the ground rice, ground almonds and sugar into a bowl.
3. Tip the egg whites into the mixer bowl. Mix on speed 1 or 2 for 10–20 seconds, then increase the speed to 4–6 and mix until fluffy with soft peaks.
4. On a low speed, slowly add the sugar mixture and mix for 10–20 seconds until thick and smooth.
5. Put small spoonfuls of the mixture spaced apart on the baking sheets – they will spread. Place a piece of glacé cherry or flaked almond in the centre of each.
6. Put into the hot oven and bake for about 15–20 minutes until pale golden.
7. Leave to cool on the baking sheet for a minute or two, and then transfer to a wire rack to cool completely, tearing round the rice paper, if using.

Pistachio Meringues

A crisp crunchy treat to go with your coffee. Often eaten on the Continent in place of a traditional biscuit.

Makes about 25

100 g/3½ oz pistachio nuts
4 large or 5 medium egg whites
200 g/7 oz golden caster sugar

1. Attach the whisk to the mixer. Line 2–3 baking sheets with baking parchment. Preheat the oven to 140°C, Fan 125°C, Gas 1.
2. Finely chop the pistachio nuts.
3. Tip the egg whites into the mixer bowl. Mix on speed 1 or 2 for 10–20 seconds, then increase the speed to 4–6 and mix until stiff peaks form.
4. On speed 4–6 slowly add half of the sugar, whisking after each addition until the meringue is stiff. Remove the bowl from the mixer. Sprinkle the remaining sugar over the surface and gently fold in to the mix with a metal spoon.
5. Put tablespoons of the mixture on the baking sheets and sprinkle with the chopped pistachio nuts.
6. Put into the hot oven and bake for about 1–2 hours, depending upon size, until crisp and dry.
7. Leave to cool on the baking sheet for a minute or two, and then transfer to a wire rack to cool completely.

Sticky Muesli Fridge Bars

A 'no-bake' recipe to keep in the fridge. Use a different type of muesli mix to change the taste of the bars each time you make them.

Makes about 16 bars or 32 small squares

4 digestive biscuits
½ lemon
225 g/8 oz dark chocolate
Half a 400 g can condensed milk
50 g/1¼ oz butter
250 g/9 oz crisp fruit muesli cereal
150 g/5½ oz sultanas

1. Attach the mixer blade to the mixer. Line the base of a 20 cm/ 8 inch square cake tin with non-stick baking paper.
2. Put the biscuits into a food (freezer) bag and crush with the back of a spoon. Finely grate the lemon rind and squeeze out the juice.
3. Break the chocolate into a microwave-proof jug and add the condensed milk and butter. Microwave on medium heat for a few seconds until the chocolate has melted. Stir well.
4. Put all the ingredients into the mixer bowl. Mix on speed 1 for 10–20 seconds or until the ingredients are thoroughly combined.
5. With a spatula scrape the chocolate mixture into the prepared tin and smooth the surface. Mark into 16 bars or 32 small squares.
6. Cover and chill in the fridge until set. Cut into bars or squares to serve. Store in the fridge.

Lavender Shortbread

Traditional wedges of shortbread, but with the delicate hint of lavender. Use the mix to make smaller biscuits and reduce the cooking time.

Makes 8 pieces

Butter for greasing
3–4 lavender leaves
140 g/5 oz plain flour
55 g/2 oz ground rice
115 g/4 oz soft butter
55 g/2 oz caster sugar plus a little extra for sprinkling

1. Attach the mixer blade to the mixer. Lightly grease an 18 cm/7 inch flan ring on a baking sheet or a shallow cake tin. Preheat the oven to 150°C, Fan 135°C, Gas 2.
2. Finely chop the lavender leaves. Sift the flour and ground rice into a bowl.
3. Put the butter and sugar into the mixer bowl. Mix on speed 1 or 2 for 10–20 seconds, then increase the speed to 3–5 and mix until light and fluffy.
4. Add the flour and chopped lavender and use the pulse setting to gather the mixture together.
5. Lift the shortbread mixture into the flan ring or cake tin. Pinch around the edge with finger and thumb and prick the surface all over with a fork. Put into the hot oven and bake for 45–55 minutes until a pale straw colour.
6. Leave in the flan ring or cake tin for 5 minutes and cut into eight wedges and sprinkle over the extra sugar.
7. Lift onto a wire rack to cool completely.

Twice-Baked Italian Biscuits

Rather similar to Italian biscotti biscuits, these are perfect for dunking into a black or milky coffee, or a glass of vin santo.

Makes 14

Oil for greasing
175 g/6 oz selection of shelled nuts such as hazelnuts, almonds, brazils or macadamia
200 g/7 oz plain flour
1 tsp baking powder
½ tsp ground anise or ground cinnamon
2 medium eggs
115 g/4 oz icing sugar
Pinch of salt
2 tsp orange zest
2 tsp clear honey

1. Attach the mixer blade to the mixer. Lightly grease an 18 cm/ 7 inch square cake tin and line the base with non-stick baking paper (you will also need a baking sheet, lightly greased). Preheat the oven to 180°C, Fan 165°C, Gas 4.
2. Roughly chop the nuts. Sift the flour, baking powder and ground anise or cinnamon into a bowl. Break the eggs into a cup.
3. Put the icing sugar and eggs into the mixer bowl. Mix on speed 1 or 2 for 10–20 seconds, then increase the speed to 3–5 and mix until light and fluffy.
4. Using the pulse setting gradually add the salt, orange zest, honey, nuts and the flour mixture. Don't over-beat the mixture which should be quite firm and dough-like.
5. Turn the mixture into the prepared tin and press level with your fingertips.
6. Put into the hot oven and bake for about 20–25 minutes until golden brown.
7. Leave in the tin for 5 minutes until firm, then turn onto a board. Cut in half and slice each piece into 2.5 cm/1 inch fingers.
8. Carefully lift the biscuits onto the baking sheet and return to the oven. Bake for a further 10–15 minutes, turning once halfway through the cooking time.
9. Leave to cool on the baking sheet for a minute or two, and then transfer to a wire rack to cool completely.

White Chocolate and Sour Cherry Cookies

Very tempting, these biscuits are crisp on the outside and chewy in the middle.

Makes about 20 depending on their size

100 g/3½ oz dried ready-to-eat sour cherries
250 g/9 oz plain flour
1 tsp baking powder
¼ tsp ground ginger
1 medium egg
125 g/4½ oz soft butter
125 g/4½ oz caster sugar
100 g/3½ oz white chocolate chips

1. Attach the mixer blade to the mixer. Line 2–3 baking sheets with baking parchment (the cookies will spread). Preheat the oven to 180°C, Fan 165°C, Gas 4.
2. Roughly chop the cherries. Sift the flour, baking powder and ginger into a bowl and break the egg into a cup.
3. Put the butter and sugar into the mixer bowl. Mix on speed 1 or 2 for 10–20 seconds, then increase the speed to 3–5 and mix until light and fluffy.
4. On a low speed, gradually add the egg to the butter mixture. Add the flour mixture, half at a time, and then mix in the cherries and chocolate chips.
5. Put heaped teaspoons of the mixture onto the baking sheets leaving plenty of room for them to spread.
6. Put into the hot oven and bake for about 12–15 minutes until golden brown.
7. Leave to cool on the tray for a minute or two until firm, and then transfer to a wire rack to cool completely.

Orange and Walnut Bites

These bite-sized biscuits are delicious. For a change, replace the orange and walnut with lemon and hazelnut halves or aniseed and pine nuts.

Makes about 20

Oil for greasing
225 g/8 oz plain flour
115 g/4 oz soft butter
115 g/4 oz caster sugar
1 medium egg yolk
1 tsp orange flower water or 2 tsp grated orange rind
60 g/2¼ oz walnut pieces

1. Attach the mixer blade to the mixer. Lightly grease 2–3 baking sheets. Preheat the oven to 180°C, Fan 165°C, Gas 4.
2. Sift the flour into the mixer bowl and add the butter, sugar, egg yolk and orange flower water or orange rind. Mix on speed 1 or 2 for 10–20 seconds, then increase the speed to 3–5 until thoroughly mixed.
3. Take heaped teaspoons of the mixture and roll into balls. Arrange on the baking sheets leaving room for them to spread and press a piece of walnut on top of each one.
4. Put into the hot oven and bake for about 10–12 minutes until golden brown.
5. Leave to cool on the tray for a minute or two, and then transfer to a wire rack to cool completely.

Chive and Chilli Oatmeal Squares

Biscuits with attitude. If the heat is too much just omit the chilli.
They are great to dunk into a soured cream dip or hummus.

Makes about 30

Oil for greasing
10 chive stalks
200 g/7 oz plain wholemeal flour
1 tsp baking powder
70 g/2½ oz medium oatmeal
200 g/7 oz soft butter
1 tsp clear honey
¼ tsp red chilli paste
Freshly milled salt and black pepper

1. Attach the mixer blade to the mixer. Lightly grease 2–3 baking sheets. Preheat the oven to 190°C, Fan 175°C, Gas 5.
2. With scissors finely snip the chives. Sift the flour and baking powder into the mixer bowl, tipping any grains left in the sieve back into the bowl. Add the oatmeal, butter, honey, chilli paste, chives and a little seasoning.
3. Mix on speed 1 for 10–20 seconds, then increase to speed 2–3 until the ingredients are combined. If too dry, add a little cold water.
4. Turn the dough onto a lightly floured surface and gently knead until smooth. Roll out to a thickness of about 5 mm/¼ inch. Cut into squares, the size you prefer. Re-roll the trimmings.
5. Lift onto the baking sheets spaced a little apart.
6. Put into the hot oven and bake for about 10–12 minutes until golden brown.
7. Leave to cool on the tray for a minute or two, and then transfer to a wire rack to cool completely.

Sesame and Parmesan Wholemeal Nibbles

Crisp cheese biscuits to eat on their own, or serve with drinks and dips.

Makes about 30

Oil for greasing
1 medium egg
200 g/7 oz plain wholemeal flour
70 g/2½ oz plain flour plus extra for rolling
Pinch salt
¼ tsp paprika pepper
200 g/7 oz soft butter
140 g/5 oz grated Parmesan cheese
Milk
2 tbsp sesame seeds

1. Attach the mixer blade to the mixer. Lightly grease 2–3 baking sheets. Preheat the oven to 190°C, Fan 175°C, Gas 5.
2. Break the egg into a cup. Sift the two flours, salt and paprika pepper into the mixer bowl, tipping any grains left in the sieve back into the bowl. Add the butter, egg and grated Parmesan.
3. Mix on speed 1 for 10–20 seconds, then increase to speed 2–3 until the ingredients are combined. If too dry, add a little cold water.
4. Turn the dough onto a lightly floured surface and gently knead until smooth. Roll out to a thickness of about 5 mm/¼ inch. Cut into shapes such as rounds, squares, fingers or other shapes with biscuit cutters. Re-roll the trimmings.
5. Lift the shapes onto the baking sheets spaced a little apart. Brush each shape with a little milk and sprinkle over a few sesame seeds.
6. Put into the hot oven and bake for about 10–12 minutes until golden brown.
7. Leave to cool on the tray for a minute or two, and then transfer to a wire rack to cool completely.

Gingerbread People

Have great fun decorating these gingerbread shapes.

Makes about 15

Oil, for greasing
1 medium egg
350 g/12 oz plain flour
1 tsp bicarbonate of soda
3 tsp ground ginger
115 g/4 oz soft butter
175 g/6 oz soft brown sugar
4 tbsp golden syrup

To decorate
Small sweets
Currants, seeds and nuts
Glacé icing

1. Attach the mixer blade to the mixer. Lightly grease one or two baking sheets. Preheat the oven to 180°C, Fan 165°C, Gas 4.
2. Break the egg into a cup.
3. Sift the flour, bicarbonate of soda and ground ginger into the mixer bowl. Add the butter and mix on speed 1 for 10–20 seconds until it looks like crumbs.
4. Add the sugar. Mix on speed 1 for a few seconds until stirred in and, with the machine running, add the egg and golden syrup. Mix until it begins to form a soft dough, but don't over-mix.
5. Turn the dough onto a lightly floured surface and gently knead until smooth. Roll out to a thickness of about 5 mm/¼ inch. Cut into shapes with biscuit cutters or thick card templates and lift onto the baking sheet spaced apart (cook them in batches). Re-roll the trimmings.
6. Put into the hot oven and bake for about 12–15 minutes until pale golden brown.
7. Leave to cool on the tray for a minute or two, and then transfer to a wire rack to cool completely.
8. When cold, decorate as you like sticking on the sweets, currants, seeds and nuts with a little glacé icing. Leave until the icing has dried.

2

SCONES AND MUFFINS

Still warm from the oven, with flavours that smell irresistible, a freshly baked batch of muffins and scones is sure to whet the appetite. Home-made scones and muffins are wonderful with morning coffee, with afternoon tea, and at just about any other time of the day as well. Once you have started making these home-made treats, you will want to keep your food mixer in action to help produce them on a regular basis.

My scone recipes are variations on traditional favourites, both sweet and savoury. Included are Cheese and Mustard Scones (see page 40), a Blueberry and Cherry Scone-Round (see page 36) and Raisin Griddle Scones (see page 32). The muffins come in several shapes and sizes; some are light and airy whilst others have a denser texture. The muffin recipes too are savoury and sweet – just try Ginger, Honey and Sunflower Seed Muffins (see page 31) or Mozzarella and Black Olive Muffins (see page 39).

For all the recipes in this chapter I have made fairly small quantities, generally 8–12 scones and 12 muffins. Of course the recipes can all be doubled up if you have plenty of mouths to feed.

Vanilla Scones

A classic scone to serve with clotted cream and fresh strawberries, or a berry conserve.

Makes 10–12

225 g/8 oz self-raising flour, plus extra
1 medium egg
1 tsp vanilla extract
1 tsp baking powder
55 g/2 oz soft butter
25 g/1 oz golden caster sugar, plus extra
About 5 tbsp milk, plus extra

1. Attach the mixer blade to the mixer. Dust a baking sheet with a little flour. Preheat the oven to 220°C, Fan 205°C, Gas 7.
2. Lightly mix the egg in a cup with the vanilla extract.
3. Sift the flour and baking powder into the mixer bowl and add the butter. Mix on speed 1 for 10–20 seconds until it looks like crumbs.
4. Add the sugar. Mix on speed 1 for a few seconds until stirred in and with the machine running add the egg and enough of the milk, a little at a time, until the mixture just begins to form a soft dough, but don't over-mix. If the mixture is too dry, add a little more milk.
5. Turn the mixture onto a lightly floured surface and gently knead until smooth. Roll out to a thickness of about 2 cm/¾ inch and cut out rounds with a 5 cm/2 inch floured cutter. Re-roll the trimmings.
6. Place the scones on the baking sheet. Brush with milk and sprinkle with a little sugar.
7. Put into the hot oven and bake for about 10–12 minutes until golden brown.
8. Leave to cool on the tray for a minute or two, and then transfer to a wire rack.

Ginger, Honey and Sunflower Seed Muffins

Muffins are so easy to make – the ingredients are mixed until just combined and slightly lumpy.

Makes 12

Oil for greasing
60 g/2¼ oz crystallized ginger
2 medium eggs
300 g/10½ oz self-raising flour
1 tsp baking powder
1 tsp ground ginger
50 g/1¾ oz light brown sugar
2 tbsp clear honey
200 ml/7 fl oz milk
4 tbsp olive oil
4 tbsp sunflower seeds

1. Attach the mixer blade to the mixer. Lightly grease 12 deep muffin tins or line with paper cases. Preheat the oven to 200°C, Fan 185°C, Gas 6.
2. Finely chop the crystallized ginger. Break the eggs into a cup.
3. Sift the flour, baking powder and ground ginger into the mixer bowl and add the sugar, honey, milk, oil and eggs.
4. Mix on speed 1 or 2 for 10–20 seconds, then increase the speed to 2–3 until just mixed. Use the pulse setting to stir the chopped crystallized ginger and half of the sunflower seeds into the mixture.
5. Spoon the mixture into the muffin cases and scatter over the remaining sunflower seeds.
6. Put into the hot oven and bake for 20–25 minutes until risen and golden brown.
7. Transfer to a wire rack and serve warm or cold.

Raisin Griddle Scones

Cooked on the hob in a griddle pan or heavy-based frying pan, these scones freeze well.

Makes about 12–15

225 g/8 oz self-raising flour, plus extra
1 medium egg
1 tsp baking powder
Pinch of salt
55 g/2 oz soft butter
1 tbsp caster sugar, plus extra
85 g/3 oz small raisins
150 ml/¼ pint milk

1. Attach the mixer blade to the mixer. You will also need a griddle pan or a heavy-based frying pan, lightly floured.
2. Break the egg into a cup.
3. Sift the flour, baking powder and salt into the mixer bowl and add the butter. Mix on speed 1 for 10–20 seconds until it looks like crumbs.
4. Add the sugar and raisins. Mix on speed 1 for a few seconds until stirred in and with the machine running add the egg and enough of the milk, a little at a time, until the mixture just begins to form a soft dough, but don't over-mix. If the mixture is too dry, add a little more milk.
5. Turn the mixture onto a lightly floured surface and gently knead until smooth. Roll out to a thickness of about 1 cm/½ inch and cut out rounds with a 6 cm/2½ inch floured cutter. Re-roll the trimmings.
6. Heat the floured pan on the hob until moderately hot. Cook the scones for 2–3 minutes on each side until golden brown and cooked through.
7. Transfer to a wire rack. Sprinkle with sugar and serve warm or cold.

Sultana and Orange Muffins

American-style muffins are larger and have a heavier texture than the more familiar small sponge cakes.

Makes 12

Oil for greasing
2 medium eggs
300 g/10½ oz self-raising flour
1 tsp baking powder
50 g/1¼ oz caster sugar
100 ml/3½ fl oz milk
100 ml/3½ fl oz natural yogurt
4 tbsp olive oil
1 tbsp grated orange rind
100 g/3½ oz sultanas

1. Attach the mixer blade to the mixer. Lightly grease 12 deep muffin tins or line with paper cases. Preheat the oven to 200°C, Fan 185°C, Gas 6.
2. Break the eggs into a cup.
3. Sift the flour and baking powder into the mixer bowl and add the sugar, milk, yogurt, oil, orange rind and eggs.
4. Mix on speed 1 or 2 for 10–20 seconds, then increase the speed to 2–3 until just mixed. Use the pulse setting to stir the sultanas into the mixture.
5. Spoon the mixture into the muffin cases.
6. Put into the hot oven and bake for 20–25 minutes until risen and golden brown.
7. Transfer to a wire rack and serve warm or cold.

Apple Drop Scones

*Best made and eaten the same day. If preferred, make with 75 g/
2¾ oz dried fruit in place of the apple.*

Makes about 15–20

1 small eating apple
1 medium egg
225 g/8 oz self-raising flour
Pinch of salt
1 tbsp caster sugar
150 ml/¼ pint milk
150 ml/¼ apple juice
Butter or oil for frying
Maple syrup, to serve
Crème fraîche, to serve

1. Attach the mixer blade to the mixer. You will also need a griddle
   pan or a heavy-based frying pan.
2. Peel, core and grate the apple. Break the egg into a cup.
3. Sift the flour and salt into the mixer bowl and add the sugar and
   egg.
4. Mixing on speed 1, slowly add the milk and apple juice to make
   a smooth batter and then mix in the grated apple.
5. Lightly grease the griddle or frying pan and heat on the hob until
   moderately hot. Drop tablespoons of the apple batter onto the hot
   surface and cook until bubbles begin to rise to the surface and
   burst. With a palette knife turn the drop scones over and cook
   until golden brown on both sides.
6. Keep the drop scones warm whilst further batches are cooked.
   Serve three or four per person, drizzled with maple syrup and
   with a spoonful of crème fraîche on the side.

Triple Choc Muffins

Very decadent, and not for those on a diet.

Makes 12

Oil for greasing
18 mini marshmallows
18 white chocolate buttons
18 milk chocolate buttons
2 medium eggs
225 g/8 oz self-raising flour
2 tbsp cocoa powder
1 tsp baking powder
50 g/1¼ oz light brown sugar
200 ml/7 fl oz milk
100 g/3½ oz soft butter

1. Attach the mixer blade to the mixer. Lightly grease 12 deep muffin tins or line with paper cases. Preheat the oven to 200°C, Fan 185°C, Gas 6.
2. Cut each marshmallow in half. Break both types of chocolate buttons in half, keeping them separate. Break the eggs into a cup.
3. Sift the flour, cocoa powder and baking powder into the mixer bowl and add the sugar, milk, butter and eggs.
4. Mix on speed 1 or 2 for 10–20 seconds, then increase the speed to 2–3 until just mixed. Use the pulse setting to stir the broken white chocolate buttons into the mixture.
5. Spoon the mixture into the muffin cases.
6. Put into the hot oven and bake for 20–25 minutes until risen and golden brown.
7. Immediately the muffins are out of the oven put some of the broken milk chocolate buttons and marshmallows on top of each muffin. The heat will soften the chocolate.
8. Leave in the tins for 10 minutes for the topping to begin to set. Transfer to a wire rack and leave to cool completely.

Blueberry and Cherry Scone-Round

Slightly faster to make than small scones, this 'break and share' scone dough is cooked as a whole round and just scored into wedges.

Makes 8 wedges

225 g/8 oz self-raising flour, plus extra
½ lemon
50 g/1¾ oz glacé cherries
1 medium egg
1 tsp baking powder
55 g/2 oz soft butter
25 g/1 oz soft brown sugar, plus extra
50 g/1¾ oz dried ready-to-eat blueberries
About 5 tbsp milk, plus extra

1. Attach the mixer blade to the mixer. Dust a baking sheet with a little flour. Preheat the oven to 220°C, Fan 205°C, Gas 7.
2. Finely grate the rind from the lemon and squeeze out the juice. Cut the glacé cherries into quarters. Break the egg into a cup.
3. Sift the flour and baking powder into the mixer bowl and add the butter. Mix on speed 1 for 10–20 seconds until it looks like crumbs.
4. Add the sugar, egg, lemon rind and juice, glacé cherries and blueberries. Mix on speed 1 for a few seconds until stirred in and with the machine running add enough of the milk, a little at a time, until the mixture just begins to form a soft dough, but don't over-mix. If the mixture is too dry, add a little more milk.
5. Turn the mix onto a lightly floured surface and gently knead until smooth. Roll out to a thickness of about 5 cm/2 inches. Shape into a round and lift onto the baking sheet. Cut into 8 wedges but leave the pieces together in a round. Brush with milk and sprinkle with a little sugar.
6. Put into the hot oven and bake for about 14–18 minutes until golden brown.
7. Leave to cool on the tray for a minute or two, and then transfer to a wire rack. Break the scone round into wedges and serve warm or cold.

Cranberry, Fudge and Pecan Muffins

Fudge gives the muffins a lovely toffee flavour.

Makes about 12

Oil for greasing
3 squares vanilla fudge
8 pecan halves
2 medium eggs
250 g/9 oz self-raising flour
1 tsp baking powder
50 g/1¾ oz light brown sugar
250 ml/9 fl oz milk
4 tbsp olive oil
60 g/2¼ oz fresh cranberries, thawed if frozen
Icing sugar, to sift

1. Attach the mixer blade to the mixer. Lightly grease 12 deep muffin tins or line with paper cases. Preheat the oven to 200°C, Fan 185°C, Gas 6.
2. Cut the fudge into small cubes and roughly chop the pecan nuts. Break the eggs into a cup.
3. Sift the flour and baking powder into the mixer bowl and add the sugar, milk, oil and eggs.
4. Mix on speed 1 or 2 for 10–20 seconds, then increase the speed to 2–3 until just mixed. Use the pulse setting to stir the fudge, chopped pecan nuts and cranberries into the mixture.
5. Spoon the mixture into the muffin cases.
6. Put into the hot oven and bake for 20–25 minutes until risen and golden brown.
7. Transfer to a wire rack and serve warm or cold, dredged with sifted icing sugar.

Wholemeal Date and Walnut Scones

Wholemeal scones have a slightly heavier and closer texture. Using a mix of wholemeal and white flour makes them a little lighter.

Makes 10–12

125 g/4½ oz self-raising flour, plus extra
50 g/1¾ oz stoned dried ready-to-eat dates
50 g/1¾ oz walnut pieces
1 medium egg
140 g/5 oz wholemeal self-raising flour
1½ tsp baking powder
Pinch of salt
100 g/3½ oz soft butter
25 g/1 oz caster sugar, plus extra
About 5 tbsp milk, plus extra

1. Attach the mixer blade to the mixer. Dust a baking sheet with a little flour. Preheat the oven to 220°C, Fan 205°C, Gas 7.
2. Roughly chop the dates and the walnut pieces. Break the egg into a cup.
3. Sift the two flours, baking powder and salt into the mixer bowl, tipping any grains left in the sieve back into the bowl, and add the butter. Mix on speed 1 for 10–20 seconds until it looks like crumbs.
4. Add the sugar, egg, dates and walnuts. Mix on speed 1 for a few seconds until stirred in and with the machine running add enough of the milk, a little at a time, until the mixture just begins to form a soft dough, but don't over-mix. If the mixture is too dry, add a little more milk.
5. Turn the mixture onto a lightly floured surface and gently knead until smooth. Roll out to a thickness of about 2 cm/¾ inch and cut out rounds with a 5 cm/2 inch floured cutter. Re-roll the trimmings.
6. Place the scones on the baking sheet. Brush with milk and sprinkle with a little sugar.
7. Put into the hot oven and bake for about 10–12 minutes until golden brown.
8. Leave to cool on the tray for a minute or two, and then transfer to a wire rack. Serve warm or cold.

Mozzarella and Black Olive Muffins

Savoury muffins are delicious served warm. You can ring the changes by using feta cheese and sun-dried tomatoes in place of the mozzarella cheese and black olives.

Makes 10–12

Oil for greasing
60 g/2¼ oz mozzarella cheese
5 stoned black olives
2 medium eggs
300 g/10/½ oz self-raising flour
1 tsp baking powder
250 ml/9 fl oz milk
4 tbsp olive oil
1 tsp chopped fresh oregano leaves

1. Attach the mixer blade to the mixer. Lightly grease 12 deep muffin tins or line with paper cases. Preheat the oven to 200°C, Fan 185°C, Gas 6.
2. Dry the mozzarella cheese on a sheet of kitchen paper and cut into small pieces. Thinly slice the olives. Break the eggs into a bowl.
3. Sift the flour and baking powder into the mixer bowl and add the milk, oil and eggs.
4. Mix on speed 1 or 2 for 10–20 seconds, then increase the speed to 2–3 until just mixed. Use the pulse setting to stir the chopped mozzarella cheese, black olives and oregano into the mixture.
5. Spoon the mixture into the muffin cases.
6. Put into the hot oven and bake for 20–25 minutes until risen and golden brown.
7. Transfer to a wire rack and serve warm.

Cheese and Mustard Scones

Use your favourite cheese in these scones and serve with pickles or chutney.

Makes 8–10

250 g/9 oz self-raising flour, plus extra
125 g/4½ oz mature Cheddar cheese
1 medium egg
1 tsp baking powder
55 g/2 oz soft butter
2 tbsp soured cream
1 tbsp wholegrain mustard
1 tbsp chopped fresh parsley
About 3–4 tbsp milk, plus extra

1. Attach the mixer blade to the mixer. Dust a baking sheet with a little flour. Preheat the oven to 220°C, Fan 205°C, Gas 7.
2. Grate the cheese, reserving half for the topping. Break the egg into a cup.
3. Sift the flour and baking powder into the mixer bowl and add the butter. Mix on speed 1 for 10–20 seconds until it looks like crumbs.
4. Add the soured cream, egg, mustard, parsley and half of the grated cheese. Mix on speed 1 for a few seconds until stirred in and with the machine running add enough of the milk, a little at a time, until the mixture just begins to form a soft dough, but don't over-mix. If the mixture is too dry, add a little more milk.
5. Turn the mixture onto a lightly floured surface and gently knead until smooth. Roll out to a thickness of about 2 cm/¾ inch and cut out rounds with a 6 cm/2½ inch floured cutter. Re-roll the trimmings.
6. Place the scones on the baking sheet. Brush with milk and sprinkle with the remaining cheese.
7. Put into the hot oven and bake for about 10–12 minutes until golden brown.
8. Leave to cool on the tray for a minute or two, and then transfer to a wire rack. Serve warm or cold.

Bacon and Onion Cornmeal Muffins

I often make these muffins in mini-muffin tins and serve warm with soups and salads.

Makes 10–12

Oil for greasing
2 rashers lean smoked back bacon
1 spring onion
2 medium eggs
225 g/8 oz self-raising flour
115 g/4 oz cornmeal
2 tsp baking powder
50 g/1¾ oz soft butter
450 ml/16 fl oz thick Greek yogurt
125 ml/4 fl oz milk

1. Attach the mixer blade to the mixer. Lightly grease 12 deep muffin tins or line with paper cases. Preheat the oven to 200°C, Fan 185°C, Gas 6.
2. Cut any rinds from the bacon rashers and finely chop. Finely chop the spring onion. Break the eggs into a cup.
3. Heat a non-stick pan and dry-fry the bacon pieces until cooked. Drain on a piece of kitchen paper.
4. Sift the flour, cornmeal and baking powder into the mixer bowl and add the butter, yogurt, milk and eggs.
5. Mix on speed 1 or 2 for 10–20 seconds, then increase the speed to 2–3 until just mixed. Use the pulse setting to stir the bacon pieces and spring onion into the mixture.
6. Spoon the mixture into the muffin cases.
7. Put into the hot oven and bake for 20–25 minutes until risen and golden brown.
8. Transfer to a wire rack and serve warm.

3

SMALL CAKES, CUPCAKES AND TRAY BAKES

Cupcakes are a perennial favourite, but they have never been so popular as they are these days. Visitors and family can be expected to ensure a steady demand for them, so keep your food mixer and other baking equipment at the ready. In this chapter you can find a tempting choice of cupcakes and other small cakes such as Flower Cupcakes (see page 53), Chocolate Raspberry Cupcakes (see page 49) and Spiced Fig Pastries (see page 51).

And then there are the tray bakes. These make for other great favourites, including Bakewell, brownies, oat-bars and iced ginger cakes. Whether cut into squares, bars or triangles, it is my experience that they just walk off the plate.

Tray bakes and cupcakes are so easy to make, and so irresistible, that you will just want to keep on baking.

Chocolate Brownies

Chocolate cake with a hint of coffee. Don't worry if the mix sinks a little; a good brownie should be slightly moist and squidgy in the middle and crisp on the top.

Makes about 16 squares or bars

Oil, for greasing
225 g/8 oz plain dark chocolate
3 medium eggs
200 g/7 oz plain flour
2 tsp baking powder
1 tbsp coffee granules
175 g/6 oz soft dark brown sugar
175 g/6 oz soft butter
3 tbsp milk
Icing sugar, to dust

1. Attach the mixer blade to the mixer. Lightly grease a 30 x 23 cm/12 x 9 inch tray-bake tin, or use a small roasting tin. Line the base and sides with non-stick baking paper. Preheat the oven to 180°C, Fan 165°C, Gas 4.
2. Break the chocolate into squares, and put into a small microwave-proof bowl. Heat for a few seconds on medium heat until melted. Break the eggs into a cup.
3. Sift the flour and baking powder into the mixer bowl and add the coffee granules, sugar, butter, milk and eggs. Mix on speed 1 for 20–30 seconds, then increase the speed and continue until thoroughly mixed, light and fluffy.
4. Pour the cooled, melted chocolate into the mixer bowl and use the pulse speed to mix it in.
5. Spoon the mixture into the prepared tin and level the surface.
6. Put into the hot oven and bake for 25–35 minutes, or until just firm in the centre.
7. Leave to cool in the tin. Lift the cake onto a board, remove the lining paper and cut into squares or bars. Dust with icing sugar.

Iced Lemon Cupcakes

Small light cakes, brightened with a blob of icing, and with a sweet as decoration.

Makes 25–30

3 medium eggs
200 g/7 oz self-raising flour
2 tsp baking powder
175 g/6 oz caster sugar
175 g/6 oz soft butter
2 tsp grated lemon rind

Icing
175 g/6 oz icing sugar
2–3 tbsp lemon curd
Small sweets, to decorate

1. Attach the mixer blade to the mixer. Line a deep 12-hole bun tin with paper cases (bake the cakes in two or three batches). Preheat the oven to 190°C, Fan 175°C, Gas 5.
2. Break the eggs into a cup.
3. Sift the flour and baking powder into the mixer bowl and add the sugar, butter, eggs and lemon rind.
4. Mix on speed 1 for 20–30 seconds, then increase the speed and continue until thoroughly mixed.
5. Spoon the mixture into the cake cases until they are half full.
6. Put into the hot oven and bake for 15–20 minutes until risen, firm and golden brown.
7. Lift the cakes onto a wire rack and leave until cold.
8. To make the icing: Sift the icing sugar into a small bowl. Stir in the lemon curd and mix to a smooth, thick icing. Add cold water if necessary.
9. With a spoon drop a blob of icing on top of each cake and decorate with a sweet.

Bakewell Slices

This uses shortcrust rather than flaky pastry.

Makes 18–24 slices

Oil, for greasing

Pastry Base
175 g/6 oz plain flour, plus extra
85 g/3 oz soft butter

Topping
2 medium eggs
200 g/7 oz self-raising flour
55 g/2 oz ground almonds
115 g/4 oz caster sugar
55 g/2 oz soft butter
60 g/2¼ oz chopped almonds
5–6 tbsp raspberry conserve

1. Attach the mixer blade to the mixer. Lightly grease a 30 x 23 cm/12 x 9 inch tray-bake tin, or use a small roasting tin. Preheat the oven to 200°C, Fan 185°C, Gas 6.
2. For the pastry base: Sift the flour and butter into the mixer bowl. Mix on speed 1 for 10–20 seconds, until like crumbs. Add 1–2 tbsp of cold water and use the pulse setting to gather the mixture together. If too dry, add a little cold water.
3. Turn the dough onto a lightly floured surface and gently knead until smooth. Chill for 30 minutes. Roll out the pastry and use to line the tin. Prick the pastry with a fork.
4. Put into the hot oven and bake for 10–15 minutes until just cooked.
5. For the topping: Break the eggs into a cup.
6. Sift the flour into the mixer bowl and add the ground almonds, sugar, butter, chopped almonds and eggs. Mix on speed 1 for 20–30 seconds, then increase the speed and continue until thoroughly mixed.
7. Spread the conserve over the base of the pastry case. Spoon the cake mixture on top and level the surface.
8. Put into the hot oven and bake for 20–30 minutes until cooked and golden brown.
9. Leave to cool in the tin. Cut into squares or bars and serve warm or cold.

Sweet Cheese and Honey Tartlets

Little cheese-cakes in lemon pastry cases.

Makes 12

Oil, for greasing

Pastry Base
225 g/8 oz plain flour, plus extra
115 g/4 oz soft butter
1 tsp grated lemon rind

Filling
2 medium eggs
175 g/6 oz half-fat soft cream cheese
55 g/2 oz caster sugar
25 g/1 oz soft butter
2 tbsp clear honey
2 tbsp crème fraîche
Icing sugar, to dust

1. Attach the mixer blade to the mixer. Lightly grease a 12-hole deep bun tin. Preheat the oven to 190°C, Fan 175°C, Gas 5.
2. For the pastry base: Sift the flour into the mixer bowl and add the butter and lemon rind. Mix on speed 1 for 10–20 seconds, until like crumbs. Add 1–2 tbsp of cold water and use the pulse setting to gather the mixture together. If too dry, add a little cold water.
3. Turn the dough onto a lightly floured surface and gently knead until smooth. Chill for 30 minutes.
4. Roll out the pastry and cut twelve 10 cm/4 inch rounds with a plain or fluted cutter, or a tea-cup. Re-roll the trimmings. Use to line the bun tin. Prick the bases of the pastry cases with a fork.
5. For the topping: Break the eggs into a cup.
6. Put all of the filling ingredients (except the crème fraîche) into the mixer bowl. Mix on speed 1 for 20–30 seconds, then increase the speed and continue until thoroughly mixed.
7. Use the pulse setting to stir the crème fraîche into the mixture.
8. Spoon the filling into the pastry cases.
9. Put into the hot oven and bake for 20–25 minutes until the filling is set and golden brown.
10. Lift the tartlets onto a wire rack and leave until cold. Dust with icing sugar.

Sticky Iced Ginger Cake

*As a variation you could add 85 g/3 oz dried fruit or sunflower seeds
to the cake mixture.*

Makes about 16–18 pieces

Oil, for greasing
3 medium eggs
200 g/7 oz self-raising flour
2 tsp ground ginger
1 tsp baking powder
1 tsp ground mixed spice
140 g/5 oz dark brown sugar
2 tbsp black treacle or golden syrup
175 g/6 oz soft butter

Decoration
225 g/8 oz icing sugar, plus extra
About 1–2 tbsp milk
140 g/5 oz toasted chopped nuts

1. Attach the mixer blade to the mixer. Lightly grease a 30 x 23 cm/
   12 x 9 inch tray-bake tin, or use a small roasting tin. Line the base
   and sides with non-stick baking paper. Preheat the oven to 180°C,
   Fan 165°C, Gas 4.
2. Break the eggs into a cup.
3. Sift the flour, ground ginger, baking powder and ground mixed
   spice into the mixer bowl and add the sugar, treacle or syrup,
   butter and eggs.
4. Mix on speed 1 for 20–30 seconds, then increase the speed and
   continue until thoroughly mixed.
5. Spoon the mixture into the prepared tin and level the surface.
6. Put into the hot oven and bake for 30–40 minutes until risen and
   firm.
7. Leave in the tin until cool, then turn out onto a wire rack and
   leave until cold.
8. To make the icing: Sift the icing sugar into a small bowl. Stir in
   the milk and mix to a smooth icing which drops off a spoon. Add
   extra milk if necessary.
9. Put a tray under the wire rack to catch any drips. With a teaspoon
   drizzle the icing over the cake. Scatter over the chopped nuts and
   leave to set. Cut into triangles, squares or bars.

Chocolate Raspberry Cupcakes

Replace the raspberries with blueberries, blackcurrants or small pieces of peach if you prefer.

Makes 25–30

140 g/5 oz fresh raspberries
3 medium eggs
175 g/6 oz self-raising flour
1 tbsp cocoa powder
1 tsp baking powder
175 g/6 oz caster sugar
175 g/6 oz soft butter
Icing sugar, to dust

1. Attach the mixer blade to the mixer. Line a deep 12-hole bun tin with paper cases. Preheat the oven to 190°C, Fan 175°C, Gas 5.
2. Halve the raspberries and break the eggs into a cup.
3. Sift the flour, cocoa powder and baking powder into the mixer bowl and add the sugar, butter and eggs.
4. Mix on speed 1 for 20–30 seconds, then increase the speed and continue until thoroughly mixed. Use the pulse setting to add the raspberries.
5. Spoon the mixture into the cake cases until they are half full.
6. Put into the hot oven and bake for 15–20 minutes until risen, firm and golden brown.
7. Lift the cakes onto a wire rack and leave until cold. Dust with icing sugar.

Peanut and Apple Cakes

The nutty texture of the peanuts and oats combined works well with the apples.

Makes about 16

Oil, for greasing
1 lemon
2 small red-skinned apples
115 g/4 oz unsalted peanuts
3 medium eggs
200 g/7 oz self-raising flour
1 tsp baking powder
85 g/3 oz porridge oats
175 g/6 oz caster sugar
175 g/6 oz soft butter

1. Attach the mixer blade to the mixer. Lightly grease a 30 x 23 cm/12 x 9 inch tray-bake tin, or use a small roasting tin. Line the base and sides with non-stick baking paper. Preheat the oven to 180°C, Fan 165°C, Gas 4.
2. Finely grate the rind from the lemon, cut in half and squeeze out the juice. Core and roughly chop the apples. Put the apple into a small bowl with the lemon rind and juice. Roughly chop the peanuts. Break the eggs into a cup.
3. Sift the flour and baking powder into the mixer bowl and add the oats, sugar, butter and eggs.
4. Mix on speed 1 for 20–30 seconds, then increase the speed and continue until thoroughly mixed. Use the pulse setting to add the peanuts, apple, lemon rind and juice.
5. Spoon the mixture into the prepared tin and level the surface.
6. Put into the hot oven and bake for 30–35 minutes until risen and firm.
7. Leave in the tin for 10 minutes, then turn onto a wire rack and leave until cold. Cut into shapes.

Spiced Fig Pastries

A disc of pastry wraps around a sweet dried-fig filling, with a hint of cardamom or ground mixed spice.

Makes about 10–12

Oil, for greasing

Pastry
225 g/8 oz plain flour, plus extra
55 g/2 oz soft butter
55 g/2 oz white fat

Filling
115 g/4 oz dried figs
55 g/2 oz soft butter
55 g/2 oz soft light brown sugar
½ tsp ground cardamom or ground mixed spice

Caster sugar for sprinkling

1. Attach the mixer blade to the mixer. Lightly grease two baking sheets. Preheat the oven to 200°C, Fan 185°C, Gas 6.
2. For the pastry: Sift the flour into the mixer bowl and add the butter and white fat. Mix on speed 1 for 10–20 seconds, until like crumbs. Add 1–2 tbsp of cold water and use the pulse setting to gather the mixture together. If too dry, add a little cold water.
3. Turn the dough onto a lightly floured surface and gently knead until smooth. Chill for 30 minutes. Roll out the pastry and cut out 10–12 rounds with a 10 cm/4 inch cutter. Re-roll the trimmings.
4. For the filling: Finely chop the figs and put into a small bowl. Stir in the butter, sugar and ground cardamom or ground mixed spice.
5. Put a teaspoon of the filling in the centre of each pastry round. Gather the pastry over the filling and pinch the edges together. Turn over and lightly press to give a flat cake.
6. Lift the pastry 'cakes' onto the baking sheets. Make three cuts in the top of each cake with a sharp knife. Brush with water and sprinkle with caster sugar.
7. Put into the hot oven and bake for 20 minutes until golden brown.
8. Transfer to a cooling rack.

Cranberry and Walnut Oat-Bars

Lots of healthy ingredients in these crunchy bars.

Makes 16 bars

Oil, for greasing
1 orange
60 g/2¼ oz dried ready-to-eat cranberries
60 g/2¼ oz walnut pieces
2 medium eggs
70 g/2½ oz plain flour
1 tsp baking powder
1 tsp ground mixed spice
175 g/6 oz rolled oats
4 tbsp olive or sunflower oil
75 g/2¾ oz soft light brown sugar
150 g carton natural yogurt
3 tbsp sesame seeds

1. Attach the mixer blade to the mixer. Lightly grease a 20 cm/ 8 inch square cake tin and line the base with non-stick baking paper. Preheat the oven to 180°C, Fan 165°C, Gas 4.
2. Finely grate the rind from the orange, cut in half and squeeze out 2 tbsp of the juice. Roughly chop the cranberries and walnuts. Break the eggs into a cup.
3. Sift the flour, baking powder and mixed spice into the mixer bowl and add the oats, oil, sugar, eggs, orange rind and juice, and yogurt.
4. Mix on speed 1 or 2 for 20–30 seconds until combined. Add the sesame seeds, cranberries and walnuts and mix on speed 2–3 until thoroughly mixed. If the mixture is too dry, add a little more orange juice.
5. Spoon the mixture into the prepared tin, smoothing and levelling the surface.
6. Put into the hot oven and bake for about 25 minutes until golden brown. Leave in the tin until firm and cut into bars or squares.
7. Carefully lift the bars or squares onto a wire rack. Leave until cold.

Flower Cupcakes

Pretty little cakes – encourage children to be creative with the decorations.

Makes 25–30

3 medium eggs
1 tsp vanilla extract
200 g/7 oz self-raising flour
1 tsp baking powder
175 g/6 oz caster sugar
175 g/6 oz soft butter

Decoration
175 g/6 oz icing sugar, plus extra
About 1–2 tbsp apple or orange juice
Small amounts of coloured ready-made fondant icing
Coloured shiny cake decoration balls

1. Attach the mixer blade to the mixer. Line a 12-hole bun tin with paper cases (bake the cakes in two or three batches). Preheat the oven to 190°C, Fan 175°C, Gas 5.
2. Lightly mix the eggs and vanilla extract in a cup.
3. Sift the flour and baking powder into the mixer bowl and add the sugar, butter and eggs.
4. Mix on speed 1 for 20–30 seconds, then increase the speed and continue until thoroughly mixed.
5. Spoon the mixture into the cake cases until they are half full.
6. Put into the hot oven and bake for 15–20 minutes until risen, firm and golden brown.
7. Lift the cakes onto a wire rack and leave until cold.
8. To decorate the cakes: Sift the icing sugar into a small bowl. Mix in sufficient apple or orange juice to give a smooth thick icing.
9. Lightly dust a board with icing sugar, and roll out the fondant icing. Cut out shapes with small cutters or thick card templates.
10. Spread a little icing on top of each cake and decorate with the fondant shapes. Press some cake decoration balls into the fondant.

Craggy Mango and Sultana Cakes

Quick to make, I always think these cakes look better the more rugged they appear.

Makes 10–12

Oil for greasing
60 g/2¼ oz dried mango
1 medium egg
225 g/8 oz self-raising flour
1 tsp baking powder
1 tsp ground ginger
115 g/4 oz soft butter
75 g/2¾ oz soft light brown sugar
60 g/2¼ oz sultanas
4 tbsp milk
Demerara sugar, for sprinkling

1. Attach the mixer blade to the mixer. Lightly grease a baking sheet. Preheat the oven to 200°C, Fan 185°C, Gas 6.
2. Finely chop the mango. Break the egg into a cup.
3. Sift the flour, baking powder and ground ginger into the mixer bowl and add the butter. Mix on speed 1 for 10–20 seconds until it looks like crumbs.
4. Add the sugar, chopped mango and sultanas. Mix on speed 1 for a few seconds until stirred in, and with the machine running add the egg and milk, a little at a time, until it forms a sticky stiff mixture. Add a little more milk, if needed.
5. Using two forks put heaped teaspoonful amounts of the mixture onto the baking sheet leaving space for them to spread. Don't smooth the mounds – they should look craggy. Sprinkle over a little demerara sugar.
6. Put into the hot oven and bake for 15–20 minutes until risen, firm and golden brown.
7. Leave to cool for 5 minutes, then carefully lift the cakes onto a wire rack to cool completely.

Wholemeal Cupcakes

Bake the cakes in batches or use double cake cases on baking sheets.

Makes 26

13 walnut halves
3 medium eggs
115 g/4 oz self-raising flour
85 g/3 oz wholemeal flour
1 tsp baking powder
175 g/6 oz dark muscovado sugar
175 g/6 oz soft butter
1 tbsp brandy or milk

1. Attach the mixer blade to the mixer. Line a deep 12-hole bun tin with paper cases (bake the cakes in two or three batches). Preheat the oven to 190°C, Fan 175°C, Gas 5.
2. Cut the walnuts in half lengthways. Break the eggs into a cup.
3. Sift the two flours and baking powder into the mixer bowl, tipping any extra grains back into the bowl, and add the sugar, butter, eggs and brandy or milk.
4. Mix on speed 1 for 20–30 seconds, then increase the speed and continue until thoroughly mixed.
5. Spoon the mixture into the cake cases until they are half full. Put a piece of walnut on top of each but don't press them into the mix.
6. Put into the hot oven and bake for 15–20 minutes until risen, firm and golden brown.
7. Lift the cakes onto a wire rack and leave until cold.

4

LARGE CAKES, FRUIT CAKES AND TEA BREADS TO SLICE

This enticing selection – fruity, nutty, sticky, crumbly, creamy, sweet and savoury – presents some classic types of fruit cakes, other large cakes and teabreads with surprising twists and some novel flavour combinations.

These cakes and teabreads will certainly look impressive when served, but they are fully achievable, and I've added hints, tips and serving suggestions to go with the recipes. Look out for Victoria Sandwich Cake with Passion Fruit Filling (see overleaf), Courgette and Orange Teabread (see page 62), Berry Cream Gateau (see page 66), Plum Crumble Cake (see page 70), and there are ten more besides.

Naturally ideal for birthday parties and other celebrations, these tempting cakes and teabreads don't need to wait for an excuse. Just start up your food mixer and follow one of these recipes on any day, at any time of the year. Your splendid cake will then turn an ordinary day into a special occasion.

Victoria Sandwich Cake with Passion Fruit Filling

A classic Victoria sandwich cake – just fill with jam or conserve and sprinkle with icing sugar. I like to use the quick all-in-one method for these types of cakes. The filling is mascarpone and passion fruit.

Makes 8–10 wedges

Oil, for greasing
4 medium eggs
225 g/8 oz self-raising flour
2 tsp baking powder
225 g/8 oz soft dark brown sugar
225 g/8 oz soft butter or margarine

Filling
2 passion fruits
175 g/6 oz mascarpone cheese
55 g/2 oz icing sugar, plus extra

1. Attach the mixer blade to the mixer. Lightly grease two 20 cm/ 8 inch sandwich tins and line the bases with non-stick baking paper or greaseproof paper. Preheat the oven to 180°C, Fan 165°C, Gas 4.
2. Break the eggs into a cup.
3. Sift the flour and baking powder into the mixer bowl and add the sugar, butter or margarine and eggs.
4. Mix on speed 1 for 20–30 seconds, then increase the speed and continue until thoroughly mixed.
5. Spoon the mixture into the prepared sandwich tins and level the surface.
6. Put into the hot oven and bake for about 25–30 minutes or until the cakes are risen, golden brown and the tops of the cakes spring back when lightly pressed.
7. Leave in the tins for 2–3 minutes, then turn out onto a wire rack and leave to cool completely.
8. To make the filling: Cut the passion fruits in half and scoop the pulp into a bowl. Mix in the mascarpone cheese and icing sugar.
9. Sandwich the cakes together with the passion fruit filling and dust the top with icing sugar.

Cherry and Almond Teabread

Cubes of almond paste or marzipan are a surprising ingredient giving a moist stickiness to this teabread.

Makes 8–10 slices

Oil, for greasing
100 g/3½ oz almond paste or marzipan
85 g/3 oz glacé cherries
3 medium eggs
225 g/8 oz self-raising flour
175 g/6 oz caster sugar
175 g/6 oz soft butter or margarine
2 tbsp milk

1. Attach the mixer blade to the mixer. Lightly grease a 900 g/2 lb loaf tin and line the base with non-stick baking paper or grease-proof paper. Preheat the oven to 180°C, Fan 165°C, Gas 4.
2. Cut the almond paste or marzipan into small cubes and quarter the glacé cherries. Break the eggs into a cup.
3. Sift the flour into the mixer bowl and add the sugar, butter or margarine, milk and eggs. Mix on speed 1 for 20–30 seconds, then increase the speed and continue until thoroughly mixed.
4. Use the pulse setting to mix in the cubes of almond paste or marzipan and the glacé cherries.
5. Spoon the mixture into the prepared loaf tin and level the surface.
6. Put into the hot oven and bake for 1–1¼ hours or until risen and golden brown: a thin skewer inserted in the centre should come out clean.
7. Leave in the tins for 10 minutes then turn out onto a wire rack and leave to cool completely.

Raisin Parkin

Keep for 3–5 days before cutting to let the flavours and texture develop.

Makes 16 squares

Oil, for greasing
175 g/6 oz black treacle
125 g/4½ oz soft butter or margarine
125 g/4½ oz dark brown sugar
1 medium egg
225 g/8 oz plain wholemeal flour
2 tsp ground ginger
2 tsp ground cinnamon
1 tsp ground mixed spice
250 g/9 oz fine oatmeal
140 g/5 oz raisins
1 tsp bicarbonate of soda
150 ml/¼ pint milk

1. Attach the mixer blade to the mixer. Lightly grease an 18 cm/ 7 inch deep square cake tin and line the base with non-stick baking paper or greaseproof paper. Preheat the oven to 180°C, Fan 165°C, Gas 4.
2. Put the treacle into a microwave-proof jug, and add the butter or margarine and sugar. Microwave on medium heat for a few seconds until the ingredients have melted. Stir well and cool slightly. Break the egg into a cup.
3. Sift the flour, ground ginger, cinnamon and mixed spice into the mixer bowl, tipping any extra grains back into the bowl, and add the oatmeal and raisins.
4. Mix on speed 1 for 20–30 seconds, then pour in the melted, cooled treacle mixture and mix until combined.
5. In a cup mix together the bicarbonate of soda and 2 tbsp of the milk. Add to the mixture along with the egg and remaining milk. Mix on speed 2–3 until thoroughly mixed.
6. With a spatula scrape the cake mixture into the prepared tin and smooth the surface.
7. Put into the hot oven and bake for 1 hour or until firm.
8. Leave in the tin for 10 minutes then turn onto a wire rack to cool completely.
9. Wrap the cake, when cold, in greaseproof paper and foil and keep for 3–7 days before cutting into squares or slice and spread with butter.

Poppy Seed and Pine Nut Madeira Cake

This buttery poppy seed Madeira cake, topped with pine nuts, is delicious with a cup of tea or coffee.

Makes 10–12 wedges

Oil, for greasing
225 g/8 oz plain flour
1½ tsp baking powder
4 medium eggs
175 g/6 oz soft butter or margarine
1 tbsp grated lemon rind
175 g/6 oz soft golden caster sugar
2 tbsp poppy seeds
3 tbsp pine nuts

1. Attach the mixer blade to the mixer. Lightly grease a 20 cm/8 inch deep cake tin and line the base with non-stick baking paper or greaseproof paper. Preheat the oven to 180°C, Fan 165°C, Gas 4.
2. Sift the flour and baking powder into a bowl. Break the eggs into a cup.
3. Put the butter or margarine, lemon rind and sugar into the mixer bowl and mix on speed 1 for 20–30 seconds, then increase the speed and beat until light and fluffy.
4. Add the eggs, a little at a time, mixing on speed 1. Add a little flour if the mixture begins to 'curdle'.
5. Use the pulse setting to mix in the poppy seeds and the remaining flour.
6. Spoon the mixture into the prepared cake tin and level the surface.
7. Put into the hot oven and bake for about 20 minutes until the surface begins to set. Scatter the pine nuts over the top of the cake and continue baking for another 45–50 minutes until the cake is risen and golden brown: a thin skewer inserted in the centre should come out clean.
8. Leave in the tin for 10 minutes then turn out onto a wire rack and leave to cool completely.

Courgette and Orange Teabread

It's now no surprise to find vegetables, such as courgettes, carrots, potatoes and beetroot, in cakes and teabreads. They give texture and colour and are always a talking point.

Makes 8–10 slices

Oil, for greasing
2 small courgettes, about 175 g/6 oz
1 small orange
3 medium eggs
250 g/9 oz self-raising flour
1 tsp baking powder
175 g/6 oz butter
175 g/6 oz soft brown sugar
175 g/6 oz raisins

1. Attach the mixer blade to the mixer. Lightly grease a 900 g/2 lb loaf tin and line the base with non-stick baking paper or grease-proof paper. Preheat the oven to 180°C, Fan 165°C, Gas 4.
2. Coarsely grate the courgettes. Finely grate the orange rind, cut in half and squeeze out 2 tbsp of juice. Break the eggs into a cup.
3. Sift the flour and baking powder into the mixer bowl. Add the remaining ingredients.
4. Mix on speed 1 for 20–30 seconds, then increase the speed and continue until thoroughly mixed.
5. Spoon the mixture into the prepared loaf tin and level the surface.
6. Put into the hot oven and bake for 1–1¼ hours or until risen, firm and golden brown.
7. Leave in the tin for 15 minutes, then turn out onto a wire rack and leave to cool completely.

Exotic Fruit Cake

A rich fruit cake packed with plump fruit soaked in tea. A fabulous cake which can be used as the basis for a festive cake – just add icing and candles. Serve a slice with a wedge of cheese.

Makes 20 slices

**300 ml/½ pint strong black tea such as Earl Grey or
  Lapsang Souchong
550 g/1 lb 4 oz mixed dried fruits such as papaya, pineapple,
  stoned dates, sultanas, raisins or cranberries
Oil, for greasing
225 g/8 oz plain flour
1½ tsp baking powder
4 medium eggs
1 tsp vanilla extract
225 g/8 oz soft butter or margarine
225 g/8 oz soft brown sugar**

1. Make the tea and pour into a bowl. Chop the fruit, if large, and stir into the hot tea. Cover and leave overnight.
2. Attach the mixer blade to the mixer. Lightly grease a 20 cm/ 8 inch deep cake tin and line the base with non-stick baking paper or greaseproof paper. Preheat the oven to 180°C, Fan 165°C, Gas 4.
3. Sift the flour and baking powder into a bowl. Lightly mix the eggs and vanilla extract in a cup. Stir in the soaked fruits – the tea should have been absorbed.
4. Put the butter or margarine and sugar into the mixer bowl and mix on speed 1 for 20–30 seconds, then increase the speed and beat until light and fluffy.
5. Add the eggs, a little at a time, mixing on speed 1. Add a little flour if the mixture begins to 'curdle'. Mix in the remaining flour.
6. Use the pulse setting to mix in the fruits until thoroughly mixed.
7. Spoon the mixture into the prepared cake tin and level the surface.
8. Put into the hot oven and bake for 1½ – 1¾ hours until the cake is risen and golden brown: a thin skewer inserted in the centre should come out clean. If the cake begins to brown too much, cover with foil.
9. Leave in the tin for 20 minutes, then turn out onto a wire rack and leave to cool completely.

Apple Sultana Cake

An all-year-round cake, moist and fruity. Serve warm or cold.

Makes 8–10 wedges

Oil, for greasing
1 lime
300 g/10½ oz cooking apples
250 g/9 oz self-raising flour
½ tsp baking powder
¼ tsp ground cloves, optional
3 medium eggs
225 g/8 oz soft butter or margarine
225 g/8 oz soft dark brown sugar
115 g/4 oz sultanas
Icing sugar, to dust

1. Attach the mixer blade to the mixer. Lightly grease a 20 cm/ 8 inch deep cake tin and line the base with non-stick baking paper or greaseproof paper. Preheat the oven to 180°C, Fan 165°C, Gas 4.
2. Finely grate the rind from the lime, cut in half and squeeze out the juice. Peel the apples, quarter and remove the cores, then coarsely grate. Put the grated apple into a bowl and stir in the lime juice and rind. Sift the flour, baking powder and ground cloves, if using, into a bowl. Break the eggs into a cup.
3. Put the butter or margarine and sugar into the mixer bowl and mix on speed 1 for 20–30 seconds, then increase the speed and beat until light and fluffy.
4. Add the eggs, a little at a time, mixing on speed 1. Add a little flour mix if the mixture begins to 'curdle'.
5. Tip in the remaining flour mix, sultanas, grated apple and lime rind and juice. Mix until thoroughly combined.
6. Spoon the mixture into the prepared cake tin and level the surface.
7. Put into the hot oven and bake for 1 hour or until the cake is firm and golden brown: a thin skewer inserted in the centre should come out clean with no uncooked cake mixture stuck to it.
8. Leave in the tin for 30 minutes, then turn out onto a wire rack and leave to cool completely.

Pineapple Teabread

A simple yet tasty teabread made with store-cupboard ingredients.

Makes 8–10 slices

Oil, for greasing
3 medium eggs
140 g can pineapple pieces in pineapple juice
175 g/6 oz plain wholemeal flour
115 g/4 oz plain flour
1 tsp baking powder
¼ tsp bicarbonate of soda
2 tsp ground ginger
55 g/2 oz caster sugar
115 g/4 oz soft butter or margarine
2 tbsp milk

Topping
2 tbsp demerara sugar
2 tbsp sesame seeds

1. Attach the mixer blade to the mixer. Lightly grease a 900 g/2 lb loaf tin and line the base with non-stick baking paper or grease-proof paper. Preheat the oven to 180°C, Fan 165°C, Gas 4.
2. Break the eggs into a bowl. Open the can of pineapple pieces but do not drain.
3. Sift the two flours, baking powder, bicarbonate of soda and ground ginger into the mixer bowl, tipping any extra grains back into the bowl. Add the remaining ingredients, except the topping ingredients.
4. Mix on speed 1 for 20–30 seconds, then increase the speed and continue until thoroughly mixed.
5. Spoon the mixture into the prepared loaf tin and level the surface.
6. For the topping: Mix the demerara sugar and sesame seeds together in a small bowl and scatter over the top of the cake mixture.
7. Put into the hot oven and bake for 1–1¼ hours or until risen, firm and golden brown.
8. Leave in the tin for 20 minutes then turn out onto a wire rack and leave to cool completely.

Berry Cream Gateau

Nutty meringue-style cake filled with your favourite fruits and whipped cream.

Makes 10–12 slices

Oil, for greasing
5 medium eggs
140 g/5 oz caster sugar
115 g/4 oz self-raising flour
3 tbsp cornflour
85 g/3 oz ground hazelnuts

Filling
300 ml/½ pint double cream
1 tbsp brandy, optional
250 g/9 oz berries: raspberries, strawberries, blackberries or
  blueberries
2–3 tbsp berry conserve
Icing sugar, to dust

1. Attach the whisk to the mixer. Lightly grease two 20 cm/8 inch deep sandwich tins and line the base with non-stick baking paper. Preheat the oven to 190°C, Fan 175°C, Gas 5.
2. Break the eggs into a bowl.
3. Pour the eggs into the mixer bowl and add the sugar. Mix on speed 1 or 2 for 10–20 seconds, then increase the speed to 4–6 and mix until soft peaks form.
4. Remove the bowl from the mixer. Sift the flour, cornflour and ground hazelnuts over the surface. Use a metal spoon to fold the ingredients together – do this in a careful figure of eight action.
5. Spoon the mixture into the prepared sandwich tins and level the surface.
6. Put into the hot oven and bake for 25–35 minutes until risen and light golden.
7. Leave in the tins until cool then carefully turn out onto a wire rack and leave to cool completely.
8. Pour the cream into the clean mixer bowl with the whisk attached and whisk on speed 4 until lightly whipped. Stir in the brandy, if using.
9. Halve or slice the berries, if large.
10. Put one of the cakes on a serving plate and spread with the berry conserve. Swirl half of the cream over the conserve and scatter over half of the berries.

11. Cover with the second cake, swirl over the remaining cream and scatter over the remaining berries. Thickly dust with icing sugar.

Walnut Polenta Cake

Hidden in the middle of the cake is a thin layer of chopped walnuts – only revealed when the cake is sliced.

Makes 8–10 wedges

Oil, for greasing
1 lemon
3 medium eggs
100 g/3½ oz walnut pieces
2 tbsp soft brown sugar
½ tsp ground mixed spice
150 g/5½ oz self-raising flour
200 g/7 oz polenta (cornmeal)
150 g/5½ oz caster sugar
200 g/7 oz soft butter or margarine

1. Attach the mixer blade to the mixer. Lightly grease a 20 cm/ 8 inch deep cake tin and line the base with non-stick baking paper or greaseproof paper. Preheat the oven to 180°C, Fan 165°C, Gas 4.
2. Finely grate the rind from the lemon, cut in half and squeeze out the juice. Break the eggs into a cup. Roughly chop the walnut pieces and put into a small bowl. Stir in the soft brown sugar and the ground mixed spice.
3. Sift the flour into the mixer bowl and add the polenta (cornmeal), caster sugar, butter or margarine, eggs and lemon rind and juice.
4. Mix on speed 1 for 20–30 seconds, then increase the speed and continue until thoroughly mixed.
5. Spoon half of the mixture into the prepared cake tin. Level the surface and sprinkle over the walnut mixture. Spoon the remaining cake mixture on top and level the surface.
6. Put into the hot oven and bake for about 25–30 minutes or until the cake is golden brown and firm.
7. Leave in the tin for 10 minutes, then turn out onto a wire rack and leave to cool completely.

Carrot and Coconut Cake

This cake freezes well without the icing. Keep in the fridge.

Makes 10–12 slices

Oil, for greasing
1 orange
175 g/6 oz carrots
2 medium eggs
225 g/8 oz self-raising flour
1 tsp baking powder
225 g/8 oz soft light brown sugar
225 g/8 oz soft butter or margarine
115 g/4 oz desiccated coconut
3 tbsp sunflower oil

Topping
140 g/5 oz cream cheese
70 g/2½ oz desiccated coconut
70 g/2½ oz icing sugar
2 tbsp orange juice or milk

1. Attach the mixer blade to the mixer. Lightly grease a 20 cm/8 inch deep cake tin and line the base with non-stick baking paper or greaseproof paper. Preheat the oven to 180°C, Fan 165°C, Gas 4.
2. Finely grate the rind from the orange, cut in half and squeeze out the juice. Peel the carrots and finely grate. Break the eggs into a cup.
3. Sift the flour and baking powder into the mixer bowl. Add the remaining ingredients, except the topping ingredients.
4. Mix on speed 1 for 20–30 seconds, then increase the speed and continue until thoroughly mixed.
5. Spoon the mixture into the prepared cake tin and level the surface.
6. Put into the hot oven and bake for 45–55 minutes or until risen, firm and golden brown.
7. Leave in the tin for 10 minutes then turn out onto a wire rack and leave to cool completely.
8. Put all the topping ingredients into a bowl and mix thoroughly. If necessary, add extra orange juice or milk to give a soft spreadable consistency.
9. Swirl the topping over the cold cake and chill.

Chocolate Torte

A cake for chocolate lovers. For added luxury, sandwich the cake with whipped cream as well as the conserve.

Makes 12–14 wedges

Oil, for greasing
3 medium eggs
175 g/6 oz plain flour
2 tsp baking powder
60 g/2¼ oz cocoa powder
175 g/6 oz caster sugar
175 g/6 oz soft butter or margarine
175 g/6 oz golden syrup

Filling and decoration
140 g/5 oz dark chocolate
4–5 tbsp apricot conserve
Small chocolate sweets or grated chocolate

1. Attach the mixer blade to the mixer. Lightly grease a 23 cm/ 9 inch cake tin and line the base with non-stick baking paper or greaseproof paper. Preheat the oven to 180°C, Fan 165°C, Gas 4.
2. Break the eggs into a cup.
3. Sift the flour and baking powder into the mixer bowl and add the remaining cake ingredients, except those for the filling and decoration.
4. Mix on speed 1 for 20–30 seconds, then increase the speed and continue until thoroughly mixed.
5. Spoon the mixture into the prepared tin and level the surface.
6. Put into the hot oven and bake for about 1¼–1½ hours or until the cake is risen and firm.
7. Leave in the tin for 10 minutes, then turn out onto a wire rack and leave to cool completely.
8. For the filling and decoration: Break the chocolate into squares and put into a microwave-proof bowl. Microwave on medium heat for a few seconds until the chocolate has melted. Cool slightly.
9. Cut the cake in half horizontally. Spread one half with the conserve and top with the other half.
10. Put the cake on a wire rack over a tray, to catch the drips. Pour over the melted chocolate letting some drizzle down the sides. Leave until almost set and decorate with sweets or grated chocolate.

Plum Crumble Cake

A simple cake to make – I've used fresh fruits, but try it with dried figs, prunes or dates.

Serves 4–6

Oil, for greasing
350 g/12 oz plums or greengages
1 medium egg
250 g/9 oz plain flour
1 tsp baking powder
175 g/6 oz soft butter or margarine
60 g/2¼ oz ground almonds
175 g/6 oz soft brown sugar

1. Attach the mixer blade to the mixer. Lightly grease a 20 cm/ 8 inch deep cake tin and line the base with non-stick baking paper or greaseproof paper. Preheat the oven to 180°C, Fan 165°C, Gas 4.
2. Halve and stone the plums or greengages and cut each half into three wedges. Break the egg into a cup.
3. Sift the flour and baking powder into the mixer bowl and add the butter or margarine. Mix on speed 1 for 10–20 seconds until it looks like crumble.
4. Add the ground almonds, sugar and egg. Mix on speed 2 for a few seconds until stirred in but still crumble-like.
5. Spoon half the crumble mixture into the prepared cake tin and arrange half of the plum or greengage wedges on top. Cover with the remaining crumble and add the remaining plums. Lightly press the mixture down.
6. Put into the hot oven and bake for 45–55 minutes until the cake is golden brown. Leave in the tin for 20 minutes, then turn out onto a wire rack and leave to cool completely.

Savoury Cheese and Onion Teabread

For days when you want an alternative to sweet cake, try this savoury teabread. Serve as is, or spread with butter.

Makes 8–10 slices

Oil, for greasing
2 spring onions
175 g/6 oz cheese, such as Cheddar, Edam or Emmenthal
100 ml/3½ fl oz olive oil
3 medium eggs
1 tsp wholegrain mustard
2 tbsp milk
225 g/8 oz self-raising flour
60 g/2¼ oz rye flour
1 tsp baking powder
1 tsp ground mixed herbs
¼ tsp freshly ground black pepper

1. Attach the mixer blade to the mixer. Lightly grease a 900 g/2 lb loaf tin and line the base with non-stick baking paper or grease-proof paper. Preheat the oven to 180°C, Fan 165°C, Gas 4.
2. Finely chop the spring onions. Coarsely grate the cheese. Pour the oil into a jug and lightly mix in the eggs, mustard and milk.
3. Sift the two flours and baking powder into the mixer bowl, tipping any extra grains back into the bowl. Add the remaining ingredients.
4. Mix on speed 1 for 20–30 seconds, then increase the speed and continue until thoroughly mixed.
5. Spoon the mixture into the prepared loaf tin and level the surface.
6. Put into the hot oven and bake for 1–1¼ hours or until risen, firm and golden brown.
7. Leave in the tin for 15 minutes, then turn out onto a wire rack and leave to cool completely.

5

PUDDINGS AND DESSERTS

Puddings are always popular. In fact, with some people I know, when they sit down to dinner, their minds are fixed on the prospect of the pudding even while tucking into their starter and their main course. For people like this, and for the rest of us too, this chapter offers a dozen irresistible puddings which can be sure to put your food mixer to excellent use.

For hot summer days, there are cool and ice-cold treats, such as Raspberry Ripple Ice-Cream (see page 79) and Cider Syllabub with Grapes (see page 75). In the depth of winter, to keep the chill at bay, indulge in Orange and Carrot Sponge Pudding (see page 85) or Chocolate Pastry Tart with Pears (see page 80). And there are perfect puddings for more temperate spring and autumn days as well.

Don't be surprised if you find yourself returning to favourites among these recipes over and over again.

Open Strawberry and Coconut Pies

Coconut adds extra crunch and crispness to the pastry.

Serves 6

Oil, for greasing

Coconut base
175 g/6 oz plain flour, plus extra
55 g/2 oz desiccated coconut
85 g/3 oz soft butter

Filling
60 g/2¼ oz caster sugar
2 tsp balsamic vinegar
500 g/1 lb 2 oz small strawberries

1. Attach the mixer blade to the mixer. Lightly grease six individual tins or dishes about 9–10 cm/3½–4 inches in diameter, such as fluted flan tins or Yorkshire pudding tins or deep muffin tins. Preheat the oven to 200°C, Fan 185°C, Gas 6.
2. For the pastry base: Sift the flour into the mixer bowl. Add the coconut and butter and mix on speed 1 for 10–20 seconds, until like crumbs. Add about 1–2 tbsp cold water and use the pulse setting to gather the mixture together. If too dry, add more water.
3. Turn the dough onto a lightly floured surface and gently knead. Chill for 30 minutes.
4. For the filling: Put the sugar, reserving 1 tbsp, and balsamic vinegar into a large bowl and mix together.
5. Hull the strawberries, and halve if large. Fold the strawberries into the sugar mixture and leave for 30 minutes for the flavours to develop, stirring once or twice.
6. Roll out the pastry, and cut out pastry rounds slightly larger than the tins. Press the pastry into the tins, but don't trim the excess pastry.
7. Fill the cases with some of the strawberry mixture. Fold the pastry over the filling, leaving some showing. Sprinkle over the remaining sugar.
8. Put into the hot oven and bake for 25–35 minutes until the pastry is cooked. Leave in the tins until warm and firm. Turn onto a wire rack and leave to cool completely.

Cider Syllabub with Grapes

A velvety dessert. In place of the cider, you could try sweet red wine, brandy, whisky or vodka.

Serves 4

1 lemon
85 g/3 oz icing sugar or caster sugar
4 tbsp cider
300 ml/½ pint double cream
225 g/8 oz seedless green grapes

1. Attach the whisk to the mixer.
2. Finely grate the rind from the lemon, cut in half and squeeze out the juice.
3. Tip the icing sugar or caster sugar into a jug and stir in the lemon rind and juice and cider. If possible, leave for 30 minutes, stirring occasionally for the sugar to dissolve.
4. Pour the cream into the mixer bowl. Mix on speed 1 or 2 for 10–20 seconds, then increase the speed to 2–3 and mix until it begins to thicken.
5. With the machine running, gradually add the lemon mixture. The mixture will be light and fluffy, but do not over-mix. Chill for 30 minutes.
6. Halve the grapes and divide between four glasses. Spoon over the syllabub and serve immediately.

Blueberry Ricotta Cake

Ricotta cheese is slightly sweet and is traditionally used in Italian desserts.

Serves 6–8

Oil, for greasing
5 medium eggs
1 lemon
1 orange
400 g/14 oz ricotta cheese
150 ml/¼ pint double cream
25 g/1 oz cornflour
55 g/2 oz caster sugar
175 g/6 oz blueberries
Maple syrup, to serve

1. Attach the whisk to the mixer. Lightly grease a 20 cm/8 inch deep flan dish or flat-bottomed ovenproof dish and line the base with non-stick baking paper. Preheat the oven to 180°C, Fan 165°C, Gas 4.
2. Separate the eggs. Finely grate the rind or zest from the lemon and orange. Cut the orange in half and squeeze out the juice.
3. Pour the egg whites into the mixer bowl. Mix on speed 1 or 2 for 10–20 seconds, then increase the speed to 5–6 and mix until stiff peaks form. Tip the whisked egg whites into a clean bowl.
4. Spoon the ricotta cheese into the mixer bowl (no need to clean) and add the double cream, lemon and orange rind, orange juice, egg yolks, cornflour and caster sugar.
5. Mix on speed 1 for 10–20 seconds, then increase the speed to 2–3 and mix until smooth. Add the whisked egg whites, and use the pulse setting to stir in.
6. Remove the bowl from the machine and stir in the blueberries. Spoon the mixture into the prepared dish.
7. Put into the hot oven and bake for 45–55 minutes, or until firm to the touch and cooked through – cover with foil if the top becomes too brown.
8. Serve warm or cold, drizzled with maple syrup.

Coffee and Mandarin Orange Hazelnut Meringue

The secret of great meringues is simple – both the bowl and the whisk must be grease-free.

Serves 6–8

Oil, for greasing
5 medium egg whites
140 g/5 oz caster sugar
½ tsp vinegar
2 tsp cornflour
85 g/3 oz ground hazelnuts

Filling
3 mandarin oranges
300 ml/½ pint double cream
1 tbsp strong black espresso coffee
Icing sugar, to dust

1. Attach the whisk to the mixer. Draw a 20 cm/8 inch circle on a piece of non-stick baking paper. Lightly grease the side you've drawn on and press onto a baking sheet. Preheat the oven to 150°C, Fan 135°C, Gas 2.
2. Pour the egg whites into the mixer bowl and add the sugar. Mix on speed 1 or 2 for 10–20 seconds, then increase the speed to 5–6 and mix for 3 minutes until stiff peaks form.
3. Add the vinegar, cornflour and ground hazelnuts and mix on speed 1 for 2–3 seconds.
4. Spoon the mixture onto the prepared baking sheet and roughly spread to fill the circle.
5. Put into the hot oven and bake for about 1 hour until the outside is crisp but the inside is slightly chewy.
6. Leave on the tray until cold, then remove the baking paper and put onto a serving plate.
7. To make the filling: Zest or grate one of the oranges to give 1 tsp. Peel the oranges, remove the segments and chop each in half.
8. Pour the cream into a clean mixer bowl with the whisk attached and whisk on speed 4 until lightly whipped.
9. Remove the bowl and fold in the coffee, orange rind and segments. Spoon onto the cold meringue. Dust with icing sugar, and serve immediately.

Blackberry Upside-Down Pudding

A great pudding for chilly days. Serve with piping hot custard.

Serves 4–6

Oil, for greasing
2 medium eggs
1 tsp vanilla extract
140 g/5 oz light brown caster sugar
250 g/9 oz blackberries, thawed if frozen
175 g/6 oz self-raising flour
115 g/4 oz butter
2 tbsp milk

1. Attach the mixer blade to the mixer. Lightly grease a 20 cm/ 8 inch deep flan tin or flat ovenproof dish and line the base with non-stick baking paper. Preheat the oven to 180°C, Fan 165°C, Gas 4.
2. Lightly mix the eggs in a cup with the vanilla extract.
3. Scatter 25 g/1 oz of the sugar over the base of the prepared tin or dish and cover with the blackberries.
4. Sift the flour into the mixing bowl. Add the remaining sugar, butter, eggs and milk. Mix on speed 1 for 20–30 seconds, then increase the speed and continue until light and fluffy.
5. Spoon the mixture over the blackberries and level the surface.
6. Put into the hot oven and bake for about 45–55 minutes until risen, golden brown and firm to the touch. Serve hot or warm.

Raspberry Ripple Ice-Cream

*Simple to make, but allow time for the freezing and mixing stages.
Freezing dulls the flavours. Make sure the basic mixture has a good
flavour by tasting the ice-cream before it is frozen. Add extra vanilla
extract, if necessary.*

Serves 6–8

**300 ml/½ pint double cream
300 ml/½ pint thick Greek yogurt
425 ml/¾ pint ready-made custard
2 tsp vanilla extract
350 g/12 oz raspberries
4 tbsp icing sugar**

1. Attach the whisk to the mixer. You need a 1.4 litre/2½ pint
   freezer container.
2. Pour the cream into the mixer bowl. Mix on speed 1 or 2 for
   10–20 seconds, then increase the speed to 2–3 and mix until it
   begins to thicken.
3. Add the yogurt, custard, and vanilla extract. Use the pulse setting
   without over-beating until smooth.
4. Spoon the custard mixture into a freezer container, cover and
   freeze for 2 hours until it begins to look mushy. Thoroughly mix
   to break up the icy bits, cover and freeze for another 1 hour.
5. Meanwhile, crush the raspberries with the icing sugar.
6. Tip the ice-cream into a bowl, mix thoroughly and spoon half
   back into the freezer container. Spoon over the crushed raspberries and carefully spoon over the remaining ice-cream. Stir
   slightly to swirl the raspberries through the ice-cream. Level the
   surface, cover and freeze until firm.

Chocolate Pastry Tart with Pears

Rich chocolate pastry gives the wow factor to any pie or tart. Keep a supply in the freezer.

Serves 4–6

Pastry Base
200 g/7 oz plain flour, plus extra
25 g/1 oz cocoa powder
Pinch ground cinnamon
175 g/6 oz soft butter
1 medium egg yolk

Filling
3 firm pears
5 tbsp apricot conserve
Icing sugar, to decorate

1. Attach the mixer blade to the mixer. Use an 18 cm/7 inch loose-bottomed flan tin. Preheat the oven to 200°C, Fan 185°C, Gas 6.
2. For the pastry base: Sift the flour, cocoa powder and ground cinnamon into the mixer bowl. Add the butter and mix on speed 1 for 10–20 seconds, until like crumbs. Tip in the egg and use the pulse setting to gather the mixture together. If too dry, add a little cold water, 1–2 tbsp.
3. Turn the dough onto a lightly floured surface and gently knead until smooth. Chill for 30 minutes.
4. For the filling: Peel the pears, quarter and remove the cores.
5. Roll out two-thirds of the pastry and use to line the flan tin.
6. Spread the conserve over the pastry base and arrange the pears on top – domed-side uppermost.
7. Roll out the remaining pastry and cut into ribbon strips. Overlap as a lattice over the filling.
8. Put into the hot oven and bake for 30–40 minutes until the pastry is cooked and the pears are tender. Dust with icing sugar and serve warm or cold.

Mango Mousse

Hardly any effort is needed to make this dessert. Make individual versions in tea cups or just spoon into glasses and leave to set.

Serves 6–8

2 tablets lemon jelly
1 medium-sized mango
300 ml/½ pint double cream
300 ml/½ pint Greek yogurt
Raspberry purée, to serve

1. Attach the mixer blade to the mixer. Put the kettle on to boil. Line a 1.2 litre/2 pint loaf tin or deep dish with cling film.
2. Tear or cut the jelly into cubes and put into a bowl. Pour over 300 ml/½ pint boiling water and stir to dissolve. Leave until almost beginning to set.
3. Peel the mango, cut in half and remove the stone. Finely chop the flesh.
4. Pour the cream and yogurt into the mixer bowl and mix on speed 1 or 2 for 10–20 seconds, then increase the speed to 3–4 and mix until soft and fluffy.
5. With the machine running, add the jelly and, when mixed in, add the chopped mango.
6. Quickly spoon into the prepared tin, level the surface and chill until set. Turn onto a plate and remove the cling film. Slice and serve with raspberry purée.

Lemon Surprise Pudding

A traditional pudding, perfect for making with a food mixer. A light sponge with lemon sauce underneath.

Serves 4

Butter, for greasing
3 medium eggs
2 large lemons
Pinch of salt
1 tbsp icing sugar
85 g/3 oz caster sugar
1 tbsp self-raising flour
200 ml/7 fl oz milk

1. Attach the mixer blade to the mixer. Lightly butter a 1 litre/ 1¾ pint deep ovenproof dish and a roasting tin to stand the dish in. Preheat the oven to 180°C, Fan 165°C, Gas 4. Put the kettle on to boil.
2. Separate the eggs. Finely grate the rind from the lemons, cut in half and squeeze out the juice. Sift the flour onto a plate.
3. Pour the egg whites and salt into the mixer bowl and mix on speed 1 or 2 for 10–20 seconds, then increase the speed to 5–6 and gradually add the icing sugar. Mix until soft peaks form. Scrape the whisked egg whites into a clean bowl.
4. Tip the egg yolks into the mixer bowl (no need to clean) and add the caster sugar. Mix on speed 3–4 for 20–30 seconds until pale and fluffy. Add the flour, lemon rind and juice and milk and mix until light and fluffy.
5. Add the whisked egg whites, and use the pulse setting to stir in. Spoon the mixture into the prepared dish.
6. Stand the dish in a roasting tin and add sufficient hot water to come half way up the sides of the dish.
7. Carefully put into the hot oven and bake for 1 hour, or until the sponge has risen and is firm to the touch.

Sultana and Lime Baked Cheesecake

A cooked cheesecake to serve cold. Ideal with fruit purée or a compôte.

Serves 6

Oil, for greasing
175 g/6 oz rich tea biscuits
2 limes
3 medium eggs
85 g/3 oz butter
55 g/2 oz caster sugar
250 g/9 oz low-fat cream cheese
150 ml/¼ pint double cream
85 g/3 oz sultanas

1. Attach the mixer blade to the mixer. Lightly grease a 20 cm/ 8 inch deep, loose-bottomed cake tin and line the base with non-stick baking paper. Preheat the oven to 190°C, Fan 175°C, Gas 5.
2. Put the biscuits into a food (freezer) bag and crush with a rolling pin. Peel a few thin strips of lime rind and reserve for decoration. Finely grate the remaining rind, cut in half and squeeze out the juice. Break the eggs into a bowl.
3. Put the butter into a microwave-proof bowl. Microwave on medium heat for a few seconds until melted. Stir in the crushed biscuits and mix thoroughly.
4. Tip the biscuit mix into the prepared tin and gently press level.
5. Pour the eggs into the mixer bowl and add the sugar, cream cheese, and the lime rind and juice. Mix on speed 1 for 10–20 seconds, then increase the speed to 2–3 and mix until smooth.
6. Pour in the double cream and sultanas and mix until combined. Spoon on top of the crumb base and level the surface.
7. Put into the hot oven and bake for 50–60 minutes or until firm to the touch – cover with foil if the top becomes too brown.
8. Run a knife round the sides to loosen and leave in the tin until cold. Scatter over the reserved lime rind.

Apple and Gooseberry Crumble

Serve with scoops of vanilla ice-cream, crème fraîche or piping hot custard. I like to make large batches of the crumble mix and freeze in food (freezer) bags. You can then scoop out the amount you need, and use from frozen.

Serves 4

3 eating apples
350 g/12 oz gooseberries, fresh or frozen
225 g/8 oz plain flour
115 g/4 oz soft butter or margarine
85 g/3 oz demerara sugar
4 tbsp elderflower syrup
2 tbsp caster sugar

1. Attach the mixer blade to the mixer. Use a 1.2 litre/2 pint ovenproof dish. Preheat the oven to 180°C, Fan 165°C, Gas 4.
2. Peel, quarter, core and slice the apples. If fresh, top and tail the gooseberries.
3. Sift the flour into the mixer bowl and add the butter or margarine. Mix on speed 1–2 for 10–20 seconds until it looks like crumble. Mix in the demerara sugar.
4. Put the apples and gooseberries into the dish. Pour over the elderflower syrup, 3 tbsp cold water, and the caster sugar, and stir together.
5. Spoon the crumble mixture over the fruit. Lightly press the mixture down.
6. Put into the hot oven and bake for 40–50 minutes until the topping is golden brown.

Orange and Carrot Sponge Pudding

A bright and golden pudding with a covering of fine orange slices encasing a light, sweet carrot sponge.

Serves 4–6

140 g/5 oz butter or margarine, plus extra
3 oranges
175 g/6 oz carrots
3 medium eggs
175 g/6 oz self-raising flour
1 tsp baking powder
1 tsp ground mixed spice
140 g/5 oz light brown caster sugar
1 tbsp syrup
2 tbsp milk
Extra syrup, to serve

1. Attach the mixer blade to the mixer. Lightly butter an 850 ml/ 1½ pint shallow ovenproof dish and line the base with non-stick baking paper or greaseproof paper. Preheat the oven to 180°C, Fan 165°C, Gas 4.
2. Thinly slice the oranges. Peel and finely grate the carrots. Break the eggs into a cup.
3. Arrange the orange slices over the base and slightly up the sides of the prepared dish.
4. Sift the flour, baking powder and ground mixed spice into the mixing bowl. Add the sugar, carrots, butter or margarine, syrup, eggs and milk.
5. Mix on speed 1 for 20–30 seconds, then increase the speed and continue until thoroughly mixed.
6. Spoon the mixture into the dish and level the surface.
7. Put into the hot oven and bake for about 45–55 minutes until risen, golden brown and firm to the touch.
8. Turn out onto a warm serving plate and serve hot or warm with warmed syrup.

6

SAVOURY PIES, TARTS, PASTRIES AND CRUMBLES

It is always exciting to cut into the flaky crust of a well-made pie to reveal the savoury filling inside. Use your trusty food mixer to produce all the different types of pastry to be found in these recipes, including a cobbler and a crumble, tartlets and pasties, as well as several pies.

The savoury filling should always be enhanced by the pastry's distinctive texture and flavour. I like to experiment with flavours, such as cornmeal pastry, herb pastry and sesame-seed pastry, but you can always customise your own pastry and add flavours to your liking. The choice is yours.

There are pies and other pastry dishes here for all occasions. If you prefer an old-fashioned meat pie, try my Pork and Apple Pie (see page 93); for a delicious starter, there is Seafood Tartlets with Almond Pastry (see page 88); and, for a lighter meal, my Chicken and Peanut Curry Slice (see page 89) goes down a treat with a glass of white wine or a cold beer.

Seafood Tartlets with Almond Pastry

You can use any seafood selection in these nutty tartlets.

Serves 6

Oil for greasing

Pastry Base
175 g/6 oz plain flour,
plus extra
Pinch of salt
85 g/3 oz soft butter
55 g/2 oz blanched chopped
almonds

Filling
1 lemon
300 g/10½ oz mixed seafood,
thawed, if frozen
Few sprigs of dill
9 cherry tomatoes
3 tbsp crème fraîche
Freshly milled black pepper
2 tsp olive oil

1. Attach the mixer blade to the mixer. Lightly grease six individual flan tins or dishes about 9–10 cm/3½–4 inches in diameter, such as fluted flan tins, Yorkshire pudding tins or deep muffin cases. Preheat the oven to 200°C, Fan 185°C, Gas 6.
2. For the pastry base: Sift the flour and salt into the mixer bowl. Add the butter and mix on speed 1 for 10–20 seconds, until like crumbs. Tip in the almonds and 1 tbsp cold water and use the pulse setting to gather the mixture together. If too dry, add a little cold water.
3. Turn the dough onto a lightly floured surface and gently knead until smooth. Chill for 30 minutes.
4. For the filling: Finely grate the rind from the lemon, cut in half and squeeze out the juice. Roughly chop the seafood, if large. Finely chop the dill and thinly slice the tomatoes.
5. In a bowl mix together the lemon rind and juice, seafood, dill, crème fraîche and a little black pepper.
6. Roll out the pastry, cut out rounds slightly larger than the tins. Line the tins with the pastry, pressing it into the tins, and trim the edges.
7. Spoon the seafood filling into the pastry cases and cover with the sliced tomatoes. Drizzle the tomatoes with a little oil and add a little black pepper.
8. Put into the hot oven and bake for 25–35 minutes until the pastry is cooked.

Chicken and Peanut Curry Slice

Put the butter in the freezer 20 minutes before you start making the pastry. It needs to be cold.

Serves 4–6

Oil, for greasing

Pastry Base
200 g/7 oz strong plain bread flour, plus extra
Pinch of salt
140 g/5 oz butter, chilled
2 tsp lemon juice

Filling
350 g/12 oz boneless, skinned chicken
115 g/4 oz unsalted peanuts
1 medium red onion
1 small red pepper
2 tbsp olive oil
2 tsp curry paste, your favourite
1 tsp bouillon powder
Freshly milled salt and pepper
Beaten egg, or milk, to brush

1. Attach the mixer blade to the mixer. Grease a baking sheet. Preheat the oven to 200°C, Fan 185°C, Gas 6.
2. For the pastry base: Sift the flour and salt into the mixer bowl. Coarsely grate the butter into the flour, stirring with a fork to coat the butter with flour. Add the lemon juice and 1 tbsp cold water and mix on speed 1 for 10 seconds until like crumbs and the mixture begins to gather together. If too dry, add a little more cold water.
3. Turn the dough onto a lightly floured surface and gently knead until smooth. Chill for 30 minutes.
4. For the filling: Finely chop the chicken. Crush the peanuts. Finely chop the onion. Cut the pepper in half, remove and discard the seeds and stalk, and finely chop.
5. Heat the oil in a frying pan, add the onion and chicken and cook until golden. Stir in the pepper, peanuts, curry paste, bouillon powder and a little seasoning. Mix well and leave to cool.
6. Roll out the pastry to an oblong about 25–35 cm/10–14 inches and put onto the baking sheet.
7. Spoon the filling down the centre of the pastry. Make cuts through the pastry on both sides of the filling to give 2 cm/¾ inch strips. Fold them over the filling, brushing with a little egg or milk. Put into the hot oven and bake for 40 minutes until the pastry is cooked and golden brown.

Sesame Pastry with Lamb and Rosemary

Classic flavour combinations in a tasty aromatic dish.

Serves 4–6

Filling
500 g/1 lb 2 oz lean boneless lamb
1 red onion
2 carrots
2 rosemary sprigs
85 g/3 oz dried ready-to-eat apricots
25 g/1 oz plain flour
Freshly milled salt and pepper
1 tbsp vegetable oil
300 ml/½ pint lamb or vegetable stock

Pastry Topping
175 g/6 oz wholemeal plain flour, plus extra
Pinch of salt
85 g/3 oz soft butter or margarine
25 g/1 oz sesame seeds plus 1 tsp extra
Beaten egg, or milk, to brush

1. Attach the mixer blade to the mixer. Use a 1.2 litre/2 pint pie dish. Preheat the oven to 190°C, Fan 175°C, Gas 5.
2. For the filling: Cut the lamb into bite-sized pieces. Finely chop the onion and carrots. Pull the rosemary leaves from the stalks and finely chop. Slice the apricots into thin strips.
3. Tip the flour into a food (freezer) bag. Add the lamb and a little seasoning. Shake the bag to lightly coat the lamb.
4. Heat the oil in a non-stick pan, then cook the onion and lamb until golden. Stir in the carrots, rosemary, apricots and stock. Bring to the boil, remove from the heat and cool.
5. For the pastry topping: Sift the flour and salt into the mixer bowl, tipping any grains back into the bowl. Add the butter or margarine and mix on speed 1 for 10–20 seconds, until like crumbs. Tip in 25 g/1 oz of sesame seeds and 1 tbsp cold water and use the pulse setting to gather the mixture together. If too dry, add a little cold water.
6. Turn the dough onto a lightly floured surface and gently knead until smooth. Chill for 30 minutes.

7. Roll out the pastry about 6 cm/2½ inches larger than the edge of the dish. To cover the edge of the pie dish, cut thin pastry strips, brush with egg or milk and press around the edge, brushing again with egg or milk.

8. Spoon the filling into the dish and lift the pastry over. Press the edges together. Make a small steam-hole in the centre. Brush the pie with egg or milk and scatter over the remaining sesame seeds.

9. Put into the hot oven and bake for 40–45 minutes until cooked through and golden brown.

Goat's Cheese and Mushroom Tart

Choose a firm goat's cheese to crumble as it adds texture to the filling. Serve with peppery salad leaves.

Serves 4

Oil, for greasing

Pastry Base
**175 g/6 oz plain flour,
   plus extra**
Pinch of salt
85 g/3 oz soft butter
1 tsp grated lemon rind

Filling
225 g/8 oz mixed mushrooms
3 medium eggs
100 g packet goat's cheese
150 ml/¼ pint double cream
150 ml/¼ pint milk
2 tbsp chopped walnuts
Freshly milled salt and pepper
**Large handful small spinach
   leaves**
1 tbsp grated Parmesan cheese

1. Attach the mixer blade to the mixer. Lightly grease a 20 cm/ 8 inch deep flan tin. Preheat the oven to 200°C, Fan 185°C, Gas 6.
2. For the pastry base: Sift the flour and salt into the mixer bowl. Add the butter and mix on speed 1 for 10–20 seconds, until like crumbs. Tip in the lemon rind and 1 tbsp cold water, and use the pulse setting to gather the mixture together. If too dry, add a little cold water.
3. Turn the dough onto a lightly floured surface and gently knead until smooth. Chill for 30 minutes.
4. For the filling: Trim the mushrooms, slicing any large ones. Lightly beat the eggs in a bowl, crumble in the goat's cheese and stir in the cream, milk, walnuts and a little seasoning, but leave the mix lumpy, not a smooth paste.
5. Roll out the pastry and use to line the flan tin. Trim any excess pastry.
6. Arrange the spinach leaves and mushrooms over the base of the pastry case. Pour the egg mixture into the flan case and sprinkle over the Parmesan cheese.
7. Put into the hot oven and bake for 30–40 minutes until the pastry is golden and the filling is set.

Pork and Apple Pie

Made in a shallow tin, it is easy to slice.

Serves 6–8

Oil, for greasing

Pastry Base
Small bunch of parsley
225 g/8 oz plain flour,
  plus extra
Pinch of salt
70 g/2½ oz butter
70 g/2½ oz white fat

Filling
1 onion
1 large cooking apple
4 rashers streaky bacon
450 g/1 lb lean, minced pork
150 ml/¼ pint good flavoured
  vegetable stock
2 tbsp apple chutney
Freshly milled salt and pepper
Beaten egg, or milk, to brush

1. Attach the mixer blade to the mixer. Lightly grease a 30 x 23 cm/12 x 9 inch small roasting tin. Preheat the oven to 200°C, Fan 185°C, Gas 6.
2. For the pastry base: Finely chop the parsley. Sift the flour and salt into the mixer bowl. Add the butter and white fat and mix on speed 1 for 10–20 seconds, until like crumbs. Add 1 tbsp of the chopped parsley and 1 tbsp cold water. Use the pulse setting to gather the mixture together. If too dry, add a little more cold water.
3. Turn the dough onto a lightly floured surface and gently knead until smooth. Chill for 30 minutes.
4. For the filling: Finely chop the onion. Peel and quarter the apple, remove the core, and finely chop. Finely chop the bacon rashers, discarding the rinds.
5. Put the onion, apple, bacon and pork into the mixer bowl. Add the remaining parsley, stock, chutney and salt and pepper. Use the pulse setting to mix the ingredients together.
6. Cut the pastry in half and roll out both pieces to fit the base tin.
7. Use one pastry sheet to cover the base of the tin. Spoon over the filling and press level. Cover with the second pastry sheet.
8. With a sharp knife make a few criss-cross cuts over the pastry top and brush with egg or milk.
9. Put on a baking sheet, and put into the hot oven. Bake for 20 minutes, then reduce the temperature to 180°C, Fan 165°C, Gas 4 and bake for a further 40 minutes until the pastry is golden brown and the filling cooked. Serve hot or cold.

Chicken and Corn with a Cornmeal Pastry Lid

Cornmeal adds a warm colour and a biscuity texture to the lid.

Serves 4

Filling
3 chicken breasts
1 courgette
3 spring onions
1 garlic clove
Small piece of fresh ginger
A small bunch of coriander
2 tbsp cornflour
1 tbsp sunflower oil
115 g/4 oz sweetcorn
300 ml/½ pint chicken stock
150 ml/¼ pint coconut milk

Freshly milled salt and
　pepper black

Pastry Topping
140 g/5 oz plain flour,
　plus extra
½ tsp baking powder
Pinch of salt
85 g/3 oz cornmeal
115 g/4 oz soft butter
Milk, for brushing

1. Attach the mixer blade to the mixer. Use a 1.2 litre/2 pint ovenproof dish. Preheat the oven to 200°C, Fan 185°C, Gas 6.
2. For the filling: Cut the chicken into thin strips. Finely chop the courgette. Slice the spring onions. Crush the garlic, grate the ginger and finely chop the coriander. Blend the cornflour in a small bowl with 2 tbsp cold water.
3. Heat the oil in a large saucepan and cook the chicken until beginning to brown. Stir in the chopped courgette and sweetcorn.
4. Pour the stock and coconut milk into the pan, stir in the garlic, ginger, coriander, spring onions, seasoning and blended cornflour. Bring just to the boil and remove from the heat. Leave to cool.
5. For the pastry topping: Sift the flour, baking powder and salt into the mixer bowl. Add the cornmeal and butter, and mix on speed 1 for 10–20 seconds, until like crumbs. Add 2 tbsp of cold water. Use the pulse setting to gather the mixture together. If too dry, add a little more cold water.
6. Turn the dough onto a lightly floured surface and roll to the size of the dish. Spoon the filling into the dish and cover with the pastry. Brush with milk.
7. Put into the hot oven and bake for 30–40 minutes until cooked through and golden brown.

Steak Wraps

Rather like Beef Wellington in miniature.

Serves 4

Oil, for greasing

Pastry Base
175 g/6 oz plain flour,
 plus extra
Pinch of salt
85 g/3 oz soft butter
¼ tsp Dijon mustard

Filling
115 g/4 oz brown mushrooms
4 fillet or sirloin beef steaks
1 tbsp olive oil
Freshly milled salt and
 black pepper
85 g/3 oz coarse pork pâté
Beaten egg, to glaze

1. Attach the mixer blade to the mixer. Lightly grease a 20 cm/ 8 inch deep baking sheet. Preheat the oven to 200°C, Fan 185°C, Gas 6.
2. For the pastry base: Sift the flour and salt into the mixer bowl. Add the butter and mustard and mix on speed 1 for 10–20 seconds, until like crumbs. Add 1–2 tbsp cold water and use the pulse setting to gather the mixture together. If too dry, add a little cold water.
3. Turn the dough onto a lightly floured surface and gently knead until smooth. Chill for 30 minutes.
4. For the filling: Finely chop the mushrooms. Trim the steaks and pat dry with kitchen paper.
5. Heat the oil in a frying pan until very hot, add the steaks and cook for 30 seconds on each side until browned. Remove and leave to cool. Put the mushrooms into the pan and cook for 1–2 minutes.
6. Roll out the pastry and cut into 4 squares, large enough to wrap around the steaks.
7. Season the steaks and place one on each piece of pastry. Spread the pâté on top and cover with the mushrooms. Brush the pastry with beaten egg, then lift the pastry over the filling. Pinch to seal, and trim any excess pastry. Re-roll the trimmings and cut out a few shapes or leaves for decoration.
8. Put the wraps onto the baking sheet, sealed side down. Brush with egg, add the decoration and brush again.
9. Put into the hot oven and bake for 15–20 minutes for rare, or 25–30 minutes for medium cooked.

Bean and Chorizo Cobbler

Cobblers are usually sweet, but this one is savoury, spicy and warming.

Serves 4

Filling	150 ml/¼ pint passata
1 onion	(sieved tomatoes)
2 celery stalks	1 tsp dried mixed herbs
2 garlic cloves	
400 g can red kidney beans	*Pastry Topping*
200 g can chickpeas	¼ red chilli (see page 11)
225 g/8 oz chorizo sausage	175 g/6 oz self-raising flour
2 tsp olive oil	Pinch of salt
425 ml/¾ pint chicken stock	55 g/2 oz soft butter
	3–4 tbsp milk

1. Attach the mixer blade to the mixer. Preheat the oven to 190°C, Fan 175°C, Gas 5.
2. For the filling: Finely chop the onion and celery. Crush the garlic. Drain the cans of red kidney beans and chickpeas, and slice the chorizo.
3. Heat the oil in a wide flameproof casserole and cook the onion, celery and chorizo until browned. Tip in the remaining ingredients for the filling. Bring to the boil, reduce the heat, cover, and cook whilst you prepare the topping.
4. For the pastry topping: Remove any seeds from the chilli and finely chop. Sift the flour and salt into the mixer bowl. Add the butter and chopped chilli and mix on speed 1 for 10–20 seconds, until like crumbs. Add 1–2 tbsp of the milk and use the pulse setting to gather the mixture together. If too dry, add a little more milk. The mixture should be soft and spoonable.
5. Put the casserole on a heat-proof surface. Carefully put spoonfuls of the pastry mixture on top.
6. Put into the hot oven and cook for 20–25 minutes until piping hot and cooked through.

Salmon Envelope

A version of Koulibiac – a pastry envelope filled with fish, rice and hard-boiled egg. Serve with soured cream and salad.

Serves 4–6

Oil, for brushing	**85 g/3 oz smoked salmon trimmings**
Pastry Base	**2 hard-boiled eggs**
1 lime	**½ small red onion**
200 g/7 oz strong plain bread flour, plus extra	**Small bunch of parsley**
Pinch of salt	**6 tbsp cooked rice**
140 g/5 oz butter, chilled	**25 g/1 oz butter, melted**
	2 tbsp fish or vegetable stock
Filling	**Freshly milled white pepper**
250 g/9 oz salmon fillet	**Beaten egg, or milk, to brush**

1. Attach the mixer blade to the mixer. Grease a baking sheet. Preheat the oven to 200°C, Fan 185°C, Gas 6.
2. Grate the rind from the lime, cut in half and squeeze out the juice. For the pastry base: Sift the flour and salt into the mixer bowl. Coarsely grate the butter into the flour, stirring with a fork to coat the butter with flour. Add 1 tbsp of the grated lime rind and 1 tbsp cold water and mix on speed 1 for 10 seconds until like crumbs and the mixture begins to gather together. If too dry, add a little more cold water.
3. Turn the dough onto a lightly floured surface and gently knead until smooth. Chill for 30 minutes.
4. For the filling: Cut the salmon into small bite-sized pieces. Finely chop the smoked salmon and the eggs. Grate or finely chop the onion. Finely chop the parsley.
5. Put the rice into a bowl and stir in the melted butter, stock, both salmons, egg, onion, remaining lime rind, lime juice and parsley. Season with pepper and mix together.
6. Roll out the pastry to about a 25–30 cm/10–12 inch square and put onto the baking sheet.
7. Pile the filling in the centre of the pastry. Brush the edges of the pastry with beaten egg or milk and lift the four corners over the filling to meet in the middle. Press and flute the edges together to seal.
8. Brush with egg or milk and put into the hot oven. Bake for 30–40 minutes until the pastry is cooked and golden brown. Cover with foil if browning too much.

Roasted Pepper and Courgette Quiche

An anytime of day dish and great with a glass of wine.

Serves 4–6

Pastry Base	**Filling**
85 g/3 oz plain flour, plus extra	1 red pepper
85 g/3 oz plain wholemeal flour	1 green pepper
Pinch of salt	4 mini courgettes
85 g/3 oz soft butter	2 tbsp vegetable oil
	2 medium eggs
	150 ml/¼ pint milk
	150 ml/¼ pint crème fraîche
	85 g/3 oz cream cheese
	Freshly milled salt and pepper

1. Attach the mixer blade to the mixer. Use a 20 cm/8 inch flan tin. Preheat the oven to 190°C, Fan 175°C, Gas 5.
2. For the pastry base: Sift both flours and the salt into the mixer bowl. Add the butter and mix on speed 1 for 10–20 seconds, until like crumbs. Add 1 tbsp cold water. Use the pulse setting to gather the mixture together. If too dry, add a little more cold water.
3. Turn the dough onto a lightly floured surface and gently knead until smooth. Chill for 30 minutes.
4. For the filling: Cut the peppers in half, remove and discard the seeds and stalk, and cut each half into 4 pieces. Cut each courgette in half lengthways.
5. Heat the oil in a griddle or frying pan, and cook the peppers and courgettes until lightly browned. Lift onto kitchen paper and cool.
6. Lightly beat the eggs in a bowl, and stir in the milk, crème fraîche, cream cheese and a little seasoning.
7. Roll out the pastry and use to line the flan tin. Trim any excess pastry.
8. Arrange the peppers and courgettes over the base of the pastry case. Pour the egg mixture into the flan case.
9. Put into the hot oven and bake for 30–40 minutes until the pastry is golden and the filling is set.

Vegetable Crumble

A good basic dish – you can vary the vegetable selection with the seasons.

Serves 4–6

Crumble Topping
200 g/7 oz plain flour
85 g/3 oz soft butter
1 tbsp chopped parsley

Filling
1 leek
1 aubergine
2 garlic cloves
3 tbsp oil
350 g/12 oz peas
400 g can chopped tomatoes
3 tbsp tomato purée
300 ml/½ pint vegetable stock
3 tbsp green pesto
Freshly milled salt and pepper
55 g/2 oz grated Cheddar cheese

1. Attach the mixer blade to the mixer. Preheat the oven to 190°C, Fan 175°C, Gas 5.
2. For the crumble topping: Sift the flour into the mixer bowl. Add the butter and parsley and mix on speed 1 for 10–20 seconds, until like crumbs.
3. For the filling: Finely chop the leek and aubergine. Crush the garlic.
4. Heat the oil in a wide flameproof casserole and cook the leek and aubergine until softened. Add the garlic, peas, tomatoes, tomato purée, stock, pesto and seasoning and bring to the boil.
5. Put the casserole onto a heat-proof surface. Spoon the crumble topping in a layer on top and sprinkle over the cheese.
6. Cover, put into the hot oven and cook for 20 minutes. Remove the lid and cook for a further 15 minutes to brown the top.

Trout and Prawn Pasties

The same size as a Cornish pastie, but stuffed full of trout and prawns.

Serve 6

Oil, for greasing

Pastry Base
250 g/9 oz plain flour,
   plus extra
Pinch of salt
55 g/2 oz soft butter
85 g/3 oz white fat

Filling
2 tbsp capers, optional
1 lemon
6 sprigs of tarragon
3 skinless, boned, ready-to-eat
   smoked trout fillets
115 g/4 oz small prawns,
   thawed, if frozen
4 tbsp tomato relish
2 tsp mild horseradish sauce
Freshly milled black pepper
Beaten egg, or milk, to brush

1. Attach the mixer blade to the mixer. Lightly grease two baking sheets. Preheat the oven to 200°C, Fan 185°C, Gas 6.
2. For the pastry base: Sift the flour and salt into the mixer bowl. Add the butter and white fat and mix on speed 1 for 10–20 seconds, until like crumbs. Add 1–2 tbsp cold water and use the pulse setting to gather the mixture together. If too dry, add a little cold water.
3. Turn the dough onto a lightly floured surface and gently knead until smooth. Chill for 30 minutes.
4. For the filling: If using, rinse the capers to remove any excess brine. Finely grate the rind from the lemon, cut in half and squeeze out the juice. Pull the tarragon leaves from the stalks and finely chop. Flake the trout into large pieces, removing any bones.
5. Put the filling ingredients into a bowl and season with pepper. Mix together with a fork.
6. Roll out the pastry and cut into 16–18 cm/6¼–7 inch rounds, using a small plate or saucer as a guide.
7. Spoon the filling onto the pastry rounds in a line down the middle. Brush the edges with egg or milk and lift over the filling. Pinch and seal the edges, and brush with egg or milk.
8. Put into the hot oven and bake for 25–35 minutes until the pastry is cooked.

7

BREADS AND PASTA

Home-made bread is well worth the effort. It smells so good and it tastes so fresh and exciting. Here are some of my favourite recipes – a selection of loaves, rolls and buns – some savoury, some sweet, some yeasty, some not. There are pizzas and pasta dishes too.

The aromas and flavours of Focaccia Tear-and-Share (see page 102), Sticky Sultana, Pistachio and Cranberry Buns (see page 104), Sunflower Seed and Tomato Cornbread (see page 114), and Apricot Cake (see page 109), straight from the oven, warm and enticing, would be just about impossible to resist.

Here are some tips to bear in mind. Leave the dough to rise in a draught-free place, which is warm but not hot. To check that your loaf is cooked, carefully turn it over, tap the bottom and it should sound hollow. If it does, the loaf is cooked. Otherwise, return it to the oven for a few more minutes. Use your food mixer to add in all those healthy ingredients which help to give each type of bread its own special character.

Focaccia Tear-and-Share

An Italian flat bread which is easy to make.

Serves 4–6

Oil, for greasing
Semolina
1 small red onion
3 rosemary sprigs
2 garlic cloves
700 g/1 lb 9 oz strong white flour, plus extra
¼ tsp salt
1½ tsp fast-action dried yeast
¼ tsp sugar
3 tbsp olive oil, plus extra
Sea salt

1. Attach the dough blade to the mixer. Lightly grease a roasting tin and sprinkle with semolina. Put the kettle on.
2. Cut the onion into quarters and thinly slice. Pull the leaves from the rosemary sprigs, and roughly chop half. Slice the garlic cloves. Pour 450 ml/¾ pint warm water (from the kettle) into a jug.
3. Sieve the flour and salt into the mixer bowl, add the yeast and sugar and mix on speed 1 for a second to combine. Add enough of the water to mix to a soft dough. If too dry, add a little more water. Add the chopped rosemary and half of the onion and garlic. Mix on speed 2 for 3 minutes until the dough is smooth.
4. Turn the dough onto a lightly floured surface and knead into a ball. Put into a bowl, loosely cover with oiled cling film and leave to rise for about 1 hour until doubled in size.
5. Gently knead the dough, to knock out the air. Roll out to roughly the size of the tin. Lift the dough into the tin and press the dough to fit the tin.
6. Scatter the remaining onion, rosemary and garlic over the surface and drizzle over 3 tbsp of oil. Using your fingertips, make deep indents all over the dough. Leave until doubled in height, about 30–40 minutes.
7. Preheat the oven to 220°C, Fan 205°C, Gas 7.
8. Put into the hot oven and bake for 15–20 minutes until golden brown and cooked through. Drizzle over a little more oil and scatter over a little sea salt. Lift onto a wire rack and leave to cool.

Herby Granary Bread

A crunchy granary loaf with a spiral of herbs running through the middle. Delicious with cheese or pâté.

Makes a 900 g/2 lb loaf

Oil, for greasing
150 ml/¼ pint milk
A small bunch of mixed herbs
450 g/1 lb granary bread flour, plus extra
1 tsp salt
1½ tsp fast-action dried yeast
2 tsp soft brown sugar
85 g/3 oz butter
2 tbsp mixed seeds, such as sunflower seeds, pumpkin seeds and sesame seeds

1. Attach the dough blade to the mixer. Lightly grease a 900 g/2 lb loaf tin.
2. Heat the milk until it is just tepid. Finely chop the herbs.
3. Put the flour and salt into the mixer bowl, add the yeast and sugar and mix on speed 1 for a second to combine. Add 25 g/1 oz of the butter and mix, until like crumbs. Add the seeds and enough of the milk to make a soft dough. If too dry, add a little more milk. Mix on speed 2 for 3 minutes until the dough is smooth.
4. Turn the dough onto a lightly floured surface and knead into a ball. Put into a bowl, loosely cover with oiled cling film and leave to rise for about 1 hour until doubled in size.
5. Gently knead the dough, to knock out the air, and roll out to an oblong 15 x 25 cm/ 6 x 10 inches.
6. Spread the butter over the dough and scatter over the chopped herbs. Roll the dough over the filling like a swiss roll. Lift into the loaf tin and loosely cover with oiled cling film. Leave to rise for about 1 hour until doubled in size.
7. Preheat the oven to 220°C, Fan 205°C, Gas 7.
8. Sprinkle a dusting of flour over the loaf. Put into the hot oven and bake for 35–45 minutes until risen and golden brown. Turn out onto a wire rack and leave to cool.

Sticky Sultana, Pistachio and Cranberry Buns

Chelsea buns with a difference. This rich dough is filled with fruits and nuts.

Makes 12

Oil, for greasing

Dough
3 medium eggs
150 ml/¼ pint milk
450 g/1 lb strong white flour, plus extra
1 tsp salt
1½ tsp fast-action dried yeast
25 g/1 oz soft brown sugar
55 g/2 oz butter

Filling
55 g/2 oz soft butter
85 g/3 oz soft brown sugar
85 g/3 oz sultanas
85 g/3 oz dried cranberries
55 g/2 oz chopped pistachio nuts or walnuts
Clear honey, for brushing

1. Attach the dough blade to the mixer. Lightly grease a roasting tin.
2. For the dough: Break the eggs into a cup. Heat the milk until it is just tepid.
3. Sieve the flour and salt into the mixer bowl, add the yeast and sugar and mix on speed 1 for a second to combine. Add the butter and mix, until like crumbs. Tip in the eggs and add enough of the milk to mix to a soft dough. If too dry, add a little more milk. Mix on speed 2 for 3 minutes until the dough is smooth.
4. Turn the dough onto a lightly floured surface and knead into a ball. Put into a bowl and loosely cover with oiled cling film. Leave for about 1 hour until doubled in size.
5. Turn the dough onto a lightly floured surface, knead to knock out the air, and roll out to a 38 cm/15 inch square.
6. For the filling: Melt or soften the butter and brush over the dough. Scatter over the sugar, sultanas, cranberries and the pistachio nuts or walnuts.
7. Roll the dough over the filling, like a swiss roll, and cut into 12 slices. Lay the slices flat and slightly spaced in the roasting tin. Loosely cover with oiled cling film and leave to rise for about 30–40 minutes until doubled in size.
8. Preheat the oven to 190°C, Fan 175°C, Gas 5.
9. Put into the hot oven and bake for 25–30 minutes until risen and golden brown. Immediately brush with a little honey. Lift onto a wire rack and leave to cool.

Breadsticks

These are great for dunking into dips or just nibbling on their own.

Makes 20–30

Oil, for greasing
450 g/1 lb strong white flour, plus extra
1 tsp salt
1½ tsp fast-action dried yeast
1 tbsp olive oil, plus extra
Sesame seeds
Poppy seeds

1. Attach the dough blade to the mixer. Lightly grease 2–3 baking sheets. Put the kettle on.
2. Pour 200 ml/7 fl oz tepid water (from the kettle) into a jug. Sieve the flour and salt into the mixer bowl, add the yeast and mix on speed 1 for a second to combine. Add the oil and enough of the water to make a soft dough. If too dry, add a little more water. Mix on speed 2 for 3 minutes until the dough is smooth.
3. Turn the dough onto a lightly floured surface and knead into a ball. Put into a bowl, loosely cover with oiled cling film and leave to rise for about 1 hour until doubled in size.
4. Gently knead the dough, to knock out the air, and roll out the dough to an oblong roughly 20 cm/8 inches wide. Cut into ribbons 20 cm x 1 cm/8 inches x ½ inch.
5. Roll and pull each ribbon of dough into thin sticks about 25 cm/ 10 inches long – they will look rustic, not evenly smooth and round.
6. Spread some sesame seeds and poppy seeds on two trays. Roll each breadstick in one of the seeds – a few will stick.
7. Put them onto the baking sheets, leaving room for them to spread. Brush or drizzle with a little oil. Cover with oiled cling film and leave to rise for 15 minutes.
8. Preheat the oven to 200°C, Fan 185°C, Gas 6.
9. Put into the hot oven and bake for 5–12 minutes, depending on the size, until golden brown. Lift onto a wire rack and leave to cool.

Mushroom Pizzas

All you need is a glass of wine and a green salad.

Makes 4 large pizzas

Oil, for greasing

Dough
450 g/1 lb oz strong white flour, plus extra
1 tsp salt
1 tsp fast-action dried yeast
2 tbsp olive oil

Topping
225 g/8 oz mozzarella cheese
5 tomatoes
6 anchovy fillets, optional
225 g/8 oz mixed mushrooms
Small bunch of oregano
8 black olives
150 ml/¼ pint passata
Small handful small spinach leaves
Freshly milled black pepper
Olive oil

1. Attach the dough blade to the mixer. Lightly grease two large baking sheets. Put the kettle on.
2. For the dough: Pour 250 ml/9 fl oz tepid water (from the kettle) into a jug. Sieve the flour and salt into the mixer bowl, add the yeast and mix on speed 1 for a second to combine. Add the oil and enough of the water to make a soft dough. If too dry, add a little more water. Mix on speed 2 for 3 minutes until the dough is smooth.
3. Turn the dough onto a lightly floured surface and knead into a ball. Put into a bowl and loosely cover with oiled cling film. Leave for about 30–40 minutes until doubled in size.
4. Knead the dough to knock out the air and cut the dough into four. On a lightly floured surface, press and shape each piece of dough roughly into an 18–20 cm/7–8 inch round and put onto baking sheets. Loosely cover with oiled cling film whilst preparing the topping.

5. Thinly slice or tear the mozzarella cheese, slice the tomatoes and cut the anchovy fillets in half, if using. Trim and slice the mushrooms. Pull the oregano leaves from the stalks and slice the olives.
6. Spread the passata over the pizza bases, leaving the edges free. Top with the spinach leaves, tomatoes and mushrooms. Add the cheese, oregano leaves, anchovy fillets, if using, sliced olives and a little black pepper. Drizzle over a little oil.
7. Preheat the oven to 200°C, Fan 185°C, Gas 6.
8. Put into the hot oven and bake for 15–20 minutes until the base is risen and browned and the topping is cooked through. Serve immediately.

Variations:

Replace the mushrooms with prawns, smoked flaked trout, drained canned artichoke hearts (quartered), salami slices or roasted red pepper.

Mini Pizzas:

Follow the recipe to step 4, then cut the dough into 8 and roll out to small thin rounds. Add the topping as above and cook for 10–12 minutes until cooked through.

Soda Bread

Eat warm on the day it's made. In place of the buttermilk use half water and half plain yogurt, or milk with a little lemon juice added. For a softer crust, wrap a tea towel around the warm cooked bread.

Serves 4

500 g/1 lb 2 oz plain white flour, plus extra
2 tsp bicarbonate of soda
1 tsp salt
55 g/2 oz butter
248 ml carton buttermilk

1. Attach the dough blade to the mixer. Put a baking sheet into the oven. Preheat the oven to 220°C, Fan 205°C, Gas 7.
2. Sift the flour, bicarbonate of soda and salt into the mixer bowl. Add the butter and mix on speed 1 for 10 seconds. Pour in the buttermilk and mix to a soft dough. If too dry, add a little more cold water. Mix on speed 2 for 1–2 minutes until the dough is smooth.
3. Turn the dough onto a lightly floured surface and shape into a round about 2.5 cm/1 inch thick.
4. Lift the dough onto the hot baking sheet and dust the top with a little flour. With a floured knife make a deep cross in the top – without cutting all the way through.
5. Put into the hot oven and bake for 25–35 minutes until the bread is risen and the crust is golden brown. Lift onto a wire rack and leave to cool.

Apricot Cake

A light yeasted fruit cake which has its origins in and around Alsace.

Serves 6–8

3 medium eggs
200 ml/7 fl oz milk, less 2 tbsp
175 g/6 oz dried ready-to-eat apricots
375 g/13 oz strong white flour, plus extra
Pinch of salt
1½ tsp fast-action dried yeast
25 g/1 oz soft brown sugar
175 g/6 oz butter
2 tbsp amaretto or milk
55 g/2 oz blanched chopped almonds
Icing sugar, to dust

1. Attach the dough blade to the mixer. Use a 20 cm/8 inch deep cake tin. Put the kettle on.
2. Break the eggs into a cup. Heat the milk until it is just tepid. Finely chop the apricots.
3. Sieve the flour and salt into the mixer bowl, add the yeast and sugar and mix on speed 1 for a second to combine. Add 115 g/ 4 oz of the butter, the eggs, apricots, milk and amaretto or milk and mix to a soft dough. Mix on speed 2 for 1–2 minutes until the dough is smooth.
4. Thickly spread the butter inside the tin – sides and base. Sprinkle the chopped almonds onto the buttered surface.
5. Tip the dough into the tin. Loosely cover with oiled cling film and leave to rise for about 1 hour until doubled in size.
6. Preheat the oven to 200°C, Fan 185°C, Gas 6.
7. Put into the hot oven and bake for 40–50 minutes until risen and golden brown and a fine skewer inserted in the centre comes out clean.
8. Turn the cake out onto a wire rack to cool. Thickly dust with icing sugar.

Seeded Rolls

This simple dough looks and tastes wonderful when made into rolls, topped with your favourite selection of seeds. I like to use different seeds on each roll.

Makes 14

Oil, for greasing

Dough
450 g/1 lb strong white flour, plus extra
225 g/8 oz wholemeal flour
1 tsp salt
2 tsp fast-action dried yeast
25 g/1 oz butter or margarine

Toppings
Beaten egg, for brushing
A selection of seeds, such as sesame, poppy, linseed, mustard, pumpkin and sunflower

1. Attach the dough blade to the mixer. Lightly grease two baking sheets. Put the kettle on.
2. For the dough: Pour 425 ml/¾ pint tepid water (from the kettle) into a jug. Sieve the two flours and salt into the mixer bowl, add the yeast and mix on speed 1 for a second to combine. Add the butter or margarine and mix, until like crumbs. Add enough of the water to make a soft dough. If too dry, add a little more water. Mix on speed 2 for 3 minutes until the dough is smooth.
3. Turn the dough onto a lightly floured surface and cut into 14 pieces. Roll each piece into a ball and put onto the baking sheets, leaving room for them to spread.
4. Cover loosely with oiled cling film and leave for about 30–40 minutes until doubled in size.
5. Preheat the oven to 200°C, Fan 185°C, Gas 6.
6. Gently brush the rolls with beaten egg and sprinkle over some seeds.
7. Put into the hot oven and bake for 25–30 minutes until risen and golden brown. Lift onto a wire rack and leave to cool.

Chocolate and Blueberry Rolls

I make these with different fillings, both sweet and savoury, including strawberries and conserve, smoked salmon and cream cheese, and cheese and mango chutney. For savoury ones, replace the vanilla extract with chopped fresh herbs.

Makes 12

Oil, for greasing

25 g/1 oz butter or margarine
1 tsp vanilla extract

Dough
675 g/1½ lb strong white flour, plus extra
1 tsp salt
2 tsp fast-action dried yeast

Filling
12 squares of dark chocolate
250 g/9 oz blueberries
Beaten egg, for brushing
Rice flakes

1. Attach the dough blade to the mixer. Lightly grease two baking sheets. Put the kettle on.
2. For the dough: Pour 425 ml/¾ pint tepid water (from the kettle) into a jug. Sieve the flour and salt into the mixer bowl, add the yeast and mix on speed 1 for a second to combine. Add the butter or margarine and mix, until like crumbs. Add the vanilla extract and enough of the water to make soft dough. If too dry, add a little more water. Mix on speed 2 for 3 minutes until the dough is smooth.
3. Turn the dough onto a lightly floured surface and knead into a ball. Put into a bowl, loosely cover with oiled cling film and leave to rise for about 1 hour until doubled in size.
4. Turn the dough onto a lightly floured surface and cut into 12 pieces. Knead and roll, then press each piece into a flat round.
5. Put a piece of chocolate in the middle of each round of dough and add a few blueberries. Brush the edges with a little egg and gather the dough over the filling, pinching the edges to seal. Gently roll into a ball and put onto the baking sheets, leaving room for them to spread.
6. Cover loosely with oiled cling film and leave for about 20–30 minutes until doubled in size.
7. Preheat the oven to 200°C, Fan 185°C, Gas 6.
8. Gently brush the rolls with beaten egg and sprinkle over some rice flakes.
9. Put into the hot oven and bake for 25–30 minutes until risen and golden brown. Lift onto a wire rack and leave to cool.

Walnut and Rye Bread

*Rye flour is low in gluten and on its own makes a very heavy dough.
So always mix with other flours.*

Serves 4–6

Oil, for greasing
140 g/5 oz walnut pieces
525 g/1 lb 3 oz strong white bread flour, plus extra
175 g/6 oz rye flour
½ tsp salt
2 tsp fast-action dried yeast
1 tbsp clear honey
1 tbsp walnut oil
1 tbsp olive oil

1. Attach the dough blade to the mixer. Lightly grease a baking sheet. Put the kettle on.
2. Roughly chop the walnuts. Pour 425 ml/¾ pint tepid water (from the kettle) into a jug.
3. Sieve the two flours and salt into the mixer bowl, add the yeast and mix on speed 1 for a second to combine. Add the chopped walnuts, honey, walnut oil, olive oil and enough of the water to mix to a soft dough. If too dry, add a little more milk. Mix on speed 2 for 3 minutes until the dough is smooth.
4. Turn the dough onto a lightly floured surface and knead into a ball. Put into a bowl, loosely cover with oiled cling film and leave to rise for about 1 hour until doubled in size.
5. Gently knead the dough, to knock out the air, and shape into a sausage about 30 cm/12 inches long. Lift onto the baking sheet and make criss-cross cuts over the top. Loosely cover with oiled cling film and leave to rise for about 30 minutes until doubled in size.
6. Preheat the oven to 220°C, Fan 205°C, Gas 7.
7. Put into the hot oven and bake for 30–35 minutes until risen and golden brown. Turn onto a wire rack and leave to cool.

Cheese Hedgehogs

Children and adults will love turning this cheese dough into animal shapes. Make caterpillars – small marble-sized balls of dough stuck together with currants for eyes, or snakes – sausage-shaped pieces of dough bent into zigzag shapes with currants for eyes.

Makes 16

Oil, for greasing
1 medium egg
85 g/3 oz Cheddar cheese
425 ml/¾ pint milk
700 g/1 lb 9 oz strong brown flour, plus extra
1 tsp salt
2 tsp fast-action dried yeast
1 tbsp vegetable oil
Beaten egg, for brushing
Currants

1. Attach the dough blade to the mixer. Lightly grease two baking sheets.
2. Break the egg into a cup. Finely grate the cheese. Heat the milk until it is just tepid.
3. Sieve the flour and salt into the mixer bowl, add the yeast and mix on speed 1 for a second to combine. Add the cheese and pour in the oil and enough of the milk to make a soft dough. If too dry, add a little more water. Mix on speed 2 for 3 minutes until the dough is smooth.
4. Turn the dough onto a lightly floured surface, knead to knock out the air, and cut into 16 pieces. Roll each piece into a ball and pull out one end for the snout. With scissors snip the dough to form spikes. Add currants for the eyes.
5. Put them onto the baking sheets, leaving room for them to spread. Cover loosely with oiled cling film and leave for about 30–40 minutes until doubled in size.
6. Gently brush the hedgehogs with beaten egg.
7. Preheat the oven to 200°C, Fan 185°C, Gas 6.
8. Put into the hot oven and bake for 25–30 minutes until risen and golden brown. Lift onto a wire rack and leave to cool.

Sunflower Seed and Tomato Cornbread

A tasty American-style bread to serve with soups, stews and casseroles.

Serves 8–10

Oil, for greasing
4 medium eggs
200 g/7 oz butter
100 g/3½ oz sun-dried tomatoes
115 g/4 oz self-raising flour
2 tsp salt
2 tsp baking powder
1 tsp bicarbonate of soda
250 g/9 oz cornmeal (polenta)
400 ml/14 fl oz buttermilk
100 g/3½ oz sunflower seeds

1. Attach the dough blade to the mixer. Lightly grease a small roasting tin about 23 cm/9 inch square, or a deep cake tin, and line the base with non-stick baking paper. Preheat the oven to 220°C, Fan 205°C, Gas 7.
2. Break the eggs into a cup. Melt the butter. Finely chop the sun-dried tomatoes.
3. Sieve the flour, salt, baking powder and bicarbonate of soda into the mixer bowl, add the cornmeal and mix on speed 1 for a second to combine. Add the eggs, butter, buttermilk, sun-dried tomatoes and sunflower seeds. Mix on speed 2 until thoroughly mixed.
4. Spoon the mixture into the prepared tin and level the surface.
5. Put into the hot oven and bake for 25–30 minutes until risen and golden brown. Lift onto a wire rack and leave to cool.

Fresh Egg Pasta with Tomato and Basil Sauce

If you can make pastry then you can make pasta. It is always exciting to make. You can customize the flavours, the shapes and the sizes of the pasta. Make batches and freeze them.

Makes about 450 g/1 lb pasta – serves 6

Pasta Dough
3 medium eggs
300 g/10½ oz '00' white flour, plus extra
Pinch of salt

Sauce
1 shallot
1 garlic clove

1 bunch of basil
450 g/1 lb cherry tomatoes
55 g/3 oz grated Parmesan or Pecorino cheese, plus extra
2 tbsp olive oil
85 g/3 oz pine nuts
150 ml/¼ pint vegetable stock
Pinch of sugar
Freshly milled salt and pepper

1. Attach the dough blade to the mixer.
2. For the pasta dough: Break the eggs into a cup.
3. Sieve the flour and salt into the mixer bowl. Add the eggs and mix on speed 1 to form a paste. Increase to speed 2 for 2–3 minutes until the dough is smooth.
4. Wrap the dough in cling film and chill for 30 minutes.
5. Turn the dough onto a lightly floured surface and roll out very thinly. Cut into thin ribbons. Spread out the pasta and leave to dry for 10–15 minutes. Cook or freeze.
6. For the sauce: Finely chop the shallot and crush the garlic. Pull the basil leaves off the stalks, halve the tomatoes and finely grate the Parmesan or Pecorino cheese.
7. Heat the oil in a pan and fry the shallot until soft, add the pine nuts, garlic and tomatoes and cook until starting to brown. Stir in the stock, sugar, half of the basil leaves and a little seasoning. Bring to the boil and simmer for 15 minutes. Stir in the remaining basil and half of the cheese. Season, if necessary.
8. Cook fresh pasta in a large pan of boiling salted water for about 2 minutes until 'al dente', drain and serve immediately with the hot sauce and the extra cheese sprinkled over.

Fresh Spinach Pasta with Prawns and Peppers

Spinach pasta is a good partner for fish and seafood.

Makes about 450 g/1 lb pasta – serves 6

Pasta Dough
3 medium eggs
Large handful small spinach
  leaves
300 g/10½ oz '00' white flour,
  plus extra
Pinch of salt

Sauce
1 lemon
1 small bunch of fennel leaves

115 g/4 oz grated Parmesan or
  Pecorino cheese, plus extra
2 red peppers
2 tbsp olive oil
150 ml/¼ pint vegetable stock
350 g/12 oz shelled prawns
Freshly milled salt and pepper
Lemon wedges, to serve

1. Attach the dough blade to the mixer.
2. For the pasta dough: Break the eggs into a cup. Finely chop the spinach leaves.
3. Sieve the flour and salt into the mixer bowl. Add the chopped spinach and mix on speed 1 to combine. Pour in the eggs and mix on speed 1 to form a paste. Increase to speed 2 for 2–3 minutes until the dough is smooth.
4. Wrap the dough in cling film and chill for 30 minutes.
5. Turn the dough onto a lightly floured surface and roll out very thinly. Cut into wide ribbons. Spread out the pasta and leave to dry for 10–15 minutes. Cook (see below) or freeze.
6. For the sauce: Finely grate the rind from half of the lemon, cut in half and squeeze out the juice from the whole lemon. Pull the fennel leaves off the stalks and finely chop. Finely grate the Parmesan or Pecorino cheese. Cut the peppers in half, remove and discard the seeds and stalks and finely chop.
7. Heat the oil in a pan and fry the peppers until soft, add the grated lemon rind and juice, stock and half the fennel. Bring to the boil and simmer for 10 minutes. Stir in the prawns and cook for 2 minutes until heated through. Add the remaining fennel and half of the cheese. Season, if necessary.
8. Cook fresh pasta in a large pan of boiling salted water for about 2 minutes until 'al dente', drain and serve immediately with the hot sauce, extra cheese sprinkled over and a lemon wedge.

8

FILLINGS, TOPPINGS, ICINGS AND SPREADS

Savoury Flavoured Butters

To use: Slice and put on the tops of steaks, kebabs, fish, shellfish, beans and vegetables.

Parsley and Lemon
Attach the mixer blade to the mixer. Put 450 g/1 lb soft butter into the mixer bowl and add 6 tbsp finely chopped parsley and 3 tsp grated lemon rind. Mix on speed 1 until smooth. Chill for 15 minutes. Spoon the mixture onto an oblong sheet of non-stick baking paper or cling film to form a sausage shape. Roll the paper or cling film over the butter mixture. Roll to give an even shape. Chill until needed, or freeze.

Variations – Replace the parsley and lemon with:
• 6 tbsp chopped basil and 140 g/5 oz chopped walnuts.
• 6 tbsp chopped mint and 3 tbsp horseradish sauce.
• 6 tbsp chopped coriander and 2 tbsp curry paste – choose your favourite.

Sweet Flavoured Butters

To use: Slice and put on the tops of hot toast, toasted muffins and griddle scones. Spread over teabread, warm brioche bread and croissants.

Apricot and Vanilla

Attach the mixer blade to the mixer. Put 450 g/1 lb soft butter into the mixer bowl and add 3 tbsp sifted icing sugar, 4 tbsp apricot conserve and 1 tsp vanilla extract. Mix on speed 1 until smooth. Chill for 15 minutes. Spoon the mixture onto an oblong sheet of non-stick baking paper or cling film to form a sausage shape. Roll the paper, or cling film over the butter mixture. Roll to give an even shape. Chill until needed or freeze.

Variations – Replace the apricot conserve and vanilla extract with:
- 3 tbsp grated orange rind and 125 g/4½ oz chopped hazelnuts.
- 2 tbsp grated lime rind and 85 g/3 oz grated crystallised ginger.
- 1 tsp ground cinnamon and 125 g/4½ oz chopped toasted almonds.

Icings, Fillings and Toppings

To use: All of these ideas can be used as icings, fillings and or toppings. Swirl over sponge cakes, teabreads, muffins and fairy cakes.

Coffee Buttercream

Attach the mixer blade to the mixer. Put 450 g/1 lb sifted icing sugar into the mixer bowl and add 175 g/6 oz soft butter sugar and 2 tbsp cold espresso coffee. Mix on speed 1 until light and fluffy. Chill until needed, or freeze.

Orange and Cream Cheese Filling

Attach the mixer blade to the mixer. Put 250 g/9 oz sifted icing sugar into the mixer bowl and add 115 g/4 oz cream cheese and the rind and juice of an orange. Mix on speed 1 for 20 seconds and then on speed 2 until light and fluffy. Chill until needed, or freeze.

Mascarpone and Maple Syrup Cream

Attach the whisk to the mixer. Spoon 175 g/6 oz mascarpone cheese into the mixer bowl and add 3 tbsp maple syrup. Whisk on speed 1 for 20 seconds. Pour in 300 ml/½ pint double cream and mix on speed 2–3 until the cream is light and fluffy, but don't over-mix. Chill until needed.

Savoury Toppings

To use: Spoon onto jacket potatoes, pancakes and flour tortillas.

Cream Cheese, Chive and Spring Onion
Attach the mixer blade to the mixer. Put 350 g/12 oz cream cheese, 3 tbsp milk, 1 bunch of chives, finely chopped, and 4 sliced spring onions into the mixer bowl and add 2 tbsp chutney and a little seasoning. Mix on speed 1 until thoroughly mixed. Chill until needed.

Green Pesto, Tuna and Soured Cream
Attach the mixer blade to the mixer. Put two drained 185 g cans of tuna into the mixer bowl and add 2 tbsp green pesto, 300 ml/½ pint soured cream and a little seasoning. Mix on speed 1 until thoroughly mixed. Chill until needed.

Tomato, Chilli and Sausage
Attach the mixer blade to the mixer. Put 350 g/12 oz finely chopped tomatoes into the mixer bowl and add 4 Frankfurter sausages, chopped, 1 tbsp tomato purée, 2 tbsp sweet chilli sauce and a little seasoning. Mix on speed 1 until thoroughly mixed. Chill until needed, and heat portions of the mixture to use.

9

EXTRAS

Shakes, Coolers and Floats

Attach the mixer blade to the mixer. Put the ingredients into the mixer bowl and mix on speed 1 for a few seconds until thoroughly combined. Some liquids may splash.

Blackcurrant Shake
300 ml/½ pint blackcurrant yogurt, 150 ml/¼ pint milk and crushed ice.

Pineapple and Coconut Cooler
400 g can chopped pineapple in juice, 150 ml/¼ pint coconut milk, 150 ml/¼ pint milk, 2 tsp clear honey and a little crushed ice.

Peach and Mango Float
4 peaches, stones removed and finely chopped, 6 scoops of vanilla ice cream, 150 ml/¼ pint mango juice and a little crushed ice.

Extra Flavour added to Cooked Vegetables

Use the food mixer to crush and mash the vegetables. I like to spoon the vegetable mixtures into individual ovenproof dishes, top with crumbs or grated cheese, and grill or bake until piping hot and cooked through.

Potato, Crème Fraîche and Red Pesto
Attach the mixer blade to the mixer. Put 900 g/2 lb hot cooked potato into the mixer bowl and add 3 tbsp red pesto and 150 ml/ ¼ pint crème fraîche. Mix on speed 1 until crushed and mixed.

Carrots, Parsnips and Walnut Oil
Attach the mixer blade to the mixer. Put 350 g/12 oz hot cooked carrots, 350 g/12 oz hot cooked parsnips and 225 g/8 oz hot cooked potato into the mixer bowl and add 1 tbsp walnut oil, 2 tbsp olive oil and a little seasoning. Mix on speed 1 until crushed and mixed.

Sweet Potatoes, Curry and Sweetcorn
Attach the mixer blade to the mixer. Put 450 g/1 lb hot cooked sweet potatoes into the mixer bowl and add 250 g/9 oz hot cooked sweetcorn, 55 g/2 oz butter, 2 tbsp milk, 1 tbsp curry paste and a little seasoning. Mix on speed 1 until crushed.

All-Purpose Savoury Mix

To use: Shape the mixture into burgers, patties and meatballs, or press around wooden or metal skewers. It's also very useful as a filling for pies and pasties or cooked as a savoury loaf.

Minced Beef with Spices

Attach the mixer blade to the mixer. Put 900 g/2 lb lean minced beef into the mixer bowl and add 1 grated onion, 2 crushed garlic cloves, 1 bunch of chopped parsley, 2 tbsp olive oil, 3 tbsp lemon juice, 1 tsp ground cinnamon and a little seasoning. Mix on speed 1–2 until thoroughly mixed. Chill until needed, or freeze.

Variations – Replace the minced beef and parsley with:
- 900 g/2 lb minced turkey and 175 g/6 oz cranberries, fresh or frozen.
- Two 400 g cans chickpeas, lightly crushed, 6 tbsp chopped coriander and 4 tbsp breadcrumbs.
- 900 g/2 lb minced lamb, 2 tbsp finely chopped rosemary leaves and 1 tbsp redcurrant jelly.

INDEX